FEAR NOT, DREAM BIG, & EXECUTE

ISBN: 978-0-692-16884-4

Fear Not, Dream Big, & Execute

Tools to Spark Your Dream and Ignite Your Follow-Through

Jeff Meyer

Foreword

Most dreams die before they ever get a chance to grow.

It's not failure that kills them. It is fear. This could be one of the reasons why "Fear not" is one of the most common commands of God to His followers in the Bible.

Because fear is real, even for leaders (especially for leaders), our dreams are usually untapped. We don't dream BIG. We dream little.

God has created you to dream. He urges you to crave your own BIG dream. You were not created to merely carry out someone else's.

You were created to live a life of service, yes, but service can be weighty if we don't unearth our own, unique, God-given vision. We'll soon be buried under expectations unless we uncover a simple rhythm that helps us implement OUR dream. In this book I want to explore these truths.

When I work with ministry professionals, Jesus-followers, and those in the help profession, I see a common two-fold pattern: 1) Christian leaders are hesitant to dream and even when they do, 2) they often fail to execute. Many have never envisioned their future with the clarity required to realize such a future. They struggle to identify and articulate a clear forward direction, and so, they adopt the expectations of others in place of their own. Eventually this hazy rudderlessness compromises their very identity. And no one can rest easy if they lack a basic foundation.

What I want to do here is spark unsettled leaders to envision their future with the clarity necessary for realization! And by giving them simple ideas they can put into practice, this book will encourage them to pursue their future with relentless determination.

This is my hope for you. And, not just for you, but for the many who will benefit from the realization of your dream.

Look, you are an influence on those around you already. As such, you may as well put in the effort to make that influence as positive as you'd like it to be.

I invite you to join me in this worthy pursuit. The lessons contained in this book come from one who is with you on the journey. It is not that I have mastered these lessons, but I have felt the benefit of continued efforts to abide by them.

If I could borrow Paul's words to the Philippians for a moment: "I don't mean to say that I have already achieved these things or that I have already reached perfection. But, I press on to possess that perfection for which Christ Jesus first possessed me" (New Living Translation, Philippians 3:12).

Yeah, it's like that.

Once the dream is sparked, execution is imperative. There is no magic bullet. Resilience and mental fortitude are needed. You will need to learn how to overcome resistance and obstacles. This little book of lessons will aid you in doing that.

So, if you could stand to diminish fear in your life and you get excited about the notion of dreaming BIG. And, you would like to work on focusing your attention, utilizing your gifts, removing distractions, and increasing your productivity, then read on.

To be a co-creator with Him for the benefit of others is life's most fulfilling purpose.

How to make this book work for you.

I have divided this book into two parts. One part is focused on discovering your dream (**Dream Sparks**). The other, on realizing the dream (**Realization Strategies**). Start wherever you find that you need the most support. If you are a discipline machine, but are not really sure where you are headed, start with Part 1. If you have a dream yet find it difficult to execute, go ahead and start with Part 2.

You may also find it more advantageous to pick and choose chapter titles that scratch an itch. These chapters are not sequential. To help with this method I have placed a checklist of chapters that you can use to mark off as you complete them.

Most importantly, take time with the contents. Sit and reflect with each lesson. Complete the exercises in the **Try This** sections. No, seriously. Commit to following through or this book could end up like every other book on your shelf. I want this book to facilitate real change in your life and that requires commitment on your part. Consider this a journal prompting, behavioral adjustment tool. We don't master something by reading it. We master by living it.

And, finally, please share your discoveries with me at [jeffmeyer.org] or drop me a note at jeff@jeffmeyer.org I would love to hear from you.

Acknowledgments

Thank you to...

my wife Amy for her eternal devotion and daily support,

my children Kyla, Jonathan, Kacie, Matt, Abbey and Alli for your interest and creativity,

my sweet Bailey, Emmersen, and Calington for your joy and steady love,

my teammates at *the Church in Madison*, for your patience, partnership, creativity, and commitment to our mission and vision,

the members of *the Church in Madison* for your patience and partnership in connecting people to life in Jesus,

my coach and friend Lynn Schoener, for her genuine interest in my life and contribution. There is no way I would be pursuing a dream like this book without her consistent encouragement,

the PLI family for your willingness to experiment and risk,

my colleagues at Auxano for your relentless commitment to clarity and the church,

my parents Ron and LouAnn Meyer, for your unconditional love and faithful witness through all my years,

Amy's parents and my second set of parents Rich and Wendy Eckart for accepting me and welcoming me into your awesome family, including entrusting me with the best gift of all, your daughter, my dearest Amy,

my siblings (on both sides) Jenni, Andy, Janelle, Donald, Steve and Vicki, Liz, Scott and Elsa,

my Launch Team for your insight and confidence,

Dan, Dan, Dan, and Dan, (crazy number of Dan's right?) Bob, Alan, Greg, Larry, Paul and Gerri for your friendship, accountability and undying support, and

the ONE and ONLY Dream-maker for allowing me to participate and share in His dream.

Table of Contents

PART 1

Dream Sparks

SPARKS

Divine triggers that elicit
unrelenting pursuits of bold endeavors

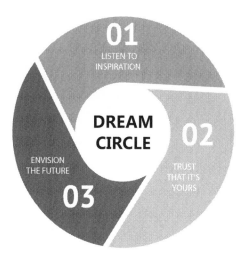

LESSON 1

Sit for a Spell

Talking Rock doesn't actually talk, but you might hear something if you sit on it long enough.

On our way back to Atlanta, somewhere near Jasper in northern Georgia, my wife Amy and I noticed a sign inviting us to turn off to "Talking Rock." We launched into a discussion about how amusing it would be if the rock actually talked, kept up conversation, made the occasional snide comment. We were in a playful mood. Pretty sure the rock doesn't talk. Unless, of course, God decided to make it talk. After all, He did make water pour out of one (see Exodus 17).

A quick search and I discovered that Talking Rock isn't a rock at all. It's a town. "Talking Rock's history is rich with stories about the Trail of Tears, the Civil War, the railroad, and the Great Depression. The origination of our town's name is unclear and there are many interesting stories regarding its derivation. Some individuals believe that it's from the noise of the water rolling over the rocks in our beautiful creek, while others like the story of folks sitting for a spell on a rock to have a talk with a neighbor. Still others believe that the name originated with the local Indians." [1]

1 *Talking Rock city website,* "*Origin of Name,*" https://www.talkingrockga.com/, (February 15, 2017).

"Sitting for a spell on a rock to talk to a neighbor." I like that explanation. Let's go with that.

You might hear something important if you sit for a spell. With a neighbor, with a friend, with your loved one, with God, even.

My friend, Greg, likes to use this formula[2] in his ministry[3] to encourage people to sit for a spell because he knows the truth of Talking Rock.

Proximity + Unhurried Time = Friendship

Draw near to God, and He will draw near to you. (English Standard Version, James 4:8).

Proximity and unhurried time. Space. Time. Intentionality and boundaries. You choose to. You create space to.

We're so busy. We're so isolated. The rhythms of our days impact friendship with others AND with God. So we have to CREATE the time and space. Abraham was described as God's friend. He created the time and space to cultivate his unique friendship with God.

It's not complicated. We get to know others better when we sit with them over time. Again and again.

---

2 Greg Finke, *Joining Jesus on His Mission: How to Be An Everyday Missionary*, (Elgin, Tyler: Tenth Power, 2014), 139.
3 Dwelling 1:14 https://dwelling114.org/

It's no wonder why so many Jesus-followers today have trouble dreaming. There is a lesson here. Sit for a spell. If we hope to discover a dream, we will need to stop and listen. Intentional space and place dedicated to listening, considering, wondering will be absolutely critical if we ever hope to discover a God-ordained dream.

We carve out time on our calendars to do all sorts of things. Schedule time to dream. Pick a morning every week. Take a day a month. Place some Talking Rock time at the beginning and end of every day. Establish space that works for you. You are free to do this. You don't need anyone else's permission. Find it. Schedule it. Don't miss your appointment.

TRY THIS

Who do you want to sit with?

When will you schedule it?

LESSON 2

People Are Not Used to Being Coached

Coaching sparks dreams.

Self-knowledge, courage to take risks, support, and focused energy are among the gifts for the individual who finds a coach. Many miss these gifts.

Most people are used to being preached at. They have grown accustomed to being told what to do. Self-knowledge is rare. The energy to think deeply, to inspect and be introspective is hard to come by. Consequently, many rely on others' answers instead of finding their own.

This is one of the main reasons why inspiring dreams are rare. And, why we tend to grind out our days working on someone else's dream instead of our own.

People expect me, as a leader, to have answers for them. Others in my professional tribe have noted such expectations and the pressure that comes along with them. The problem with providing answers for people is that it's not helping them grow. It's not helping them dream.

People are like sheep, the Scriptures say. Sheep don't have their own best answers. They are led. They are taught. They are shepherded. Sheep don't dream. (Why, then, are we supposed to count them to help us sleep? Hmmmmm...)

I believe this line of thinking about sheep leads many to expect another to give them answers. And through the years has led the shepherds to settle for giving answers. Leaders too often tell their followers what to do instead of inspiring them to find their own way.

I get it. I really do. I understand what the Scriptures say about the human condition. I concur that through the ages God has sent prophets, leaders, pastors, evangelists, teachers, parents, kings, and all those in authority. And He's doing it today. Yet, there is a way to respect and obey these authorities without becoming proverbial sheep.

Yes, my Good Shepherd restores my soul. He guides me along streams of living water...for His name's sake. And, those who faithfully lead will help us live out our unique calling and fulfill our purpose. God has never intended for us to be puppets on a string, blindly marching along to carry out the desires of magistrates. He has placed leaders and guides in our lives to redirect, realign, and realize our contribution FOR HIS NAME'S SAKE.

Simply being told what to do is not working to help people to grow. Preaching alone is not assisting people to own their dream. Nor is it yielding behavioral transformation in pursuit of those divine imprints.

The lack of interested supporters in our lives and in the lives of the people we influence is keeping people dependent on the expert. Perhaps you even picked up this book because you thought it might give you access to some golden dream nugget. I hate to disappoint.

You can access the Creator, your Creator. You can discover your dream without an intermediary placed over you simply telling you what you should do or how you should live. God has created you with your own Divine Dreams in your DNA. The best guidance comes from people who help you discover your own answers as you seek God.

Even looking at our expert leader, Jesus, whose Word is life, we can see this lesson lived out. Jesus is not merely an itinerant preacher who directs our steps. He is a soul-stirrer who invites us to walk with Him.

If our master, Jesus, leads us by walking with us and stirring us to discover, then these earthly leaders must learn to come alongside and help others discover their own best answers. Our leaders and "experts" must become experts in helping those they serve discover how to listen to the true Expert, and here's the key, FOR THEMSELVES. That is, IF we want to see people increasingly apply what they learn. If we want people to dream.

If fear keeps people from dreaming, then fear can also keep our leaders from helping others dream. Fears that individuals' dreams may conflict with the leader's dream. Fears that they are actually ill-equipped to guide people. Fears that this kind of "alongside partnership" is too demanding and intimate. Fears that they will be found as lacking any dream of their own. Telling people what they should do or think allows leaders to keep a certain relational distance.

The ability to dream belongs to everyone. In order to unleash this great movement of dreamers we, as leaders, will need to effect a shift. This shift will require of us to...

- Ask powerful, soul-stirring questions instead of giving quick expert answers, encouraging each person to find his/ her own way.
- Exhibit patience and commitment to long-term, enduring relationships.
- Transform teaching environments from transactional events to self-discovery adventures.
- Allow our Teacher/Trainer the space to ask us the powerful, soul-stirring questions that will unlock transformational discoveries for ourselves.
- Temper our defensiveness; we must learn to listen to what others say, take constructive criticism, get outside our own heads and consider other perspectives.
- Appreciate virtues like "singularity of vision" and stick-to-it-iveness in our leaders without necessarily adopting all of their answers as our own.

There are two sides to this lesson. The side that you are on when you live as a leader to another. And the side that you live on as you are influenced by other leaders. On one side of the equation the question stands: "Will you allow yourself to be coached?" On the other side there is a similar question: "Will you redirect your energies to coach others?" Both are humbling propositions.

Let us devote ourselves to helping others follow Jesus. And in the process of placing them in His care, help them discover their dream and pursue it with freedom and boldness.

TRY THIS

Here are three actionable steps you could take to increase your coaching capacity.

1. Pick a favorite coaching question and make it your own. Memorize it. Put it in your own words. Put it in your coaching tool belt. Here's a few to choose from:

    - *Say more about that? Can you expand on that?*
    - *What have you tried so far?*
    - *If nothing changes, what is likely to happen?*
    - *What ideas do you have that you'd be willing to act on?*
    - *What would you do if you weren't afraid?*
    - *If all things change when we do, what do you want to change first?*
    - *Have you checked your assumptions about that?*

2. Consider getting a coach for yourself.

3. Shift teaching environments to self-discovery adventures. Every teaching environment can be transformed. They can shift from passive learning moments to active learning spaces with simple adjustments. Here are a few examples:

- Instead of simply telling which Scripture passages to look up to make your point, make your point and then let people search for their own supporting Scripture.
- Instead of pulling out a few points in an article that you want to use to make your point, let a small group read the article for themselves and pull out the points they see as key to the discussion.
- Include a take-home exercise to try at home in your speech/sermon/class. And check in during the next class/sermon/speech to get feedback on the exercise.
- Stop right in the middle of your lecture and have the group pair up and actually do the thing you are espousing. For example, if you want them to look at the meaning of their name to gain insight about their calling or personality, then have them do it right there in that moment.

Jesus Is Your Point of Reference and Your Peace of Mind

As I write this, I just signed up for a race called Ragnar. It's a 200-mile road relay race that you run as a part of a team of twelve. It has a specific route with some sections tougher than others. Team members take portions based on their ability. Each teammate runs three portions, totaling at least twelve miles over a 24-hour period.

There are a lot of unknowns. I don't know how my body will feel on race day. I have no idea what the weather will be. At this point, five months before the race, I only know one of my teammates. I don't know what kind of runners they are or how they will respond to the challenge. As I understand it, I am the lone rookie on the team. They've all run other Ragnars. So, I can lean on their experience. I'm sure it will take great endurance. I've never run back-to-back-to-back 10k's before.

To compensate for all of this ignorance, I possess something invaluable, a critical point of reference, a map. I look at the map and see the route, distance, location, and elevation all neatly delineated. I know where we are headed. Sure, there will be twists and turns along the way, but if I study the map, I can anticipate every bend in the road and even the slightest incline.

In like manner, I coach myself to fix my eyes on Jesus. In the beginning, when I am trying to discover my dream, in the middle, when I'm tempted to quit, and at the end, when achievement is within reach... I must focus my attention on Jesus.

Let us run with endurance the race God has set before us. We do this by keeping our eyes on Jesus, the champion who initiates and perfects our faith (Hebrews 12:1-2).

Once a dream has been sparked, the way will be marked out for you, one step after another, as long as our eyes are fixed on Jesus. He both blazes the trail and smooths the path. He is the One who initiates and sustains our life of faith. He is the One who sparks and helps us realize the dream.

On a deep sea fishing excursion off the Atlantic Coast I learned a valuable lesson. It was simple. Keep your eyes focused on the horizon. Don't stare at the waves or look down. Do this and you won't get sick. It worked. Three-foot waves did not shake me. Unlike some of the others on board, I kept nausea at bay.

Keep your eyes focused on Jesus as you pursue the dream and you will get your sea legs, you will stay even-keeled.

I lift up my eyes to the hills. From where does my help come? My help comes from the Lord, who made heaven and earth (English Standard Version, Psalm 121).

But I must confess something. Most days I find it difficult to maintain my focus on God. I catch myself looking down over the edge of the boat at the waves.

My mind is frequently scattered and distracted. Any attempt to concentrate seems absurd. I can't make my mind do anything it doesn't want to do. Random thoughts pop in and join the dissonant chorus. Jumbled with words, images, and memories, my mind spins. I struggle to orient myself.

It's as if I've lost my map.

For the Christian leader, dreaming BIG, dreaming CLEARLY starts with a liberated mind. That mind, cleared of its clutter and released to soar with God, is a remarkable place of creativity.

You and I are not doomed to our usual self-defeating patterns. We can break free. And that freedom comes from God. He is your mind's creator. He is the source of your mind's freedom. He is your crucial point of reference. He will show you the way and keep you balanced.

Sounds great. But, *"How do I do this,"* you may be asking? Like all of the Christian life, one must apply this lesson through intentional and disciplined practice. Consider the following spiritual practices: the 3 M's.

Marinate

Sit with shorter sections of Scripture long enough that your mind settles and fresh insights from the Word reveal themselves. I use a methodology called 30 Things. I first learned of it in the Introduction to Timothy Keller's book, "Encounters With Jesus: Unexpected

Answers to Life's Biggest Questions."[4] It's quite simple. Sit with the short passage for 30 minutes and write down 30 things. They can be any combination of questions, observations, and insights. Then, pick one or two that really stand out to you.

I rarely gain deep insight from God instantly. I have to earn it. Knowledge and discernment emerge only with time. They reside below the surface underneath layers of assumption. In order to uncover what is buried, I will need to sit and contemplate for a while.

The key here is time.

This is why I use the word, *marinate*. Meat must sit and rest awhile in the spices to assimilate them. In order for steak or chicken to soak in the spice and be really affected by the special sauce, it needs to be immersed in it. It's the same for our minds. We have become accustomed to instant gratification. We must master the art of abiding. Pause. Linger. Tarry. Wait. Stick around. Remain. Dwell. It would be of great benefit for us as Christian leaders to marinate.

Memorize

I remember well my confirmation experience back in the late 1970's. Attending my father's confirmation class was quite formative in many ways. One way in particular was all the memorization: long passages of scripture committed to memory before I could move on to the next section of the catechism. He assigned one page of 50 passages per part of Luther's Small Catechism. I practiced at home, usually

4 Timothy Keller, introduction to *Encounters With Jesus: Unexpected Answers to Life's Biggest Questions.* (New York: Penguin, 2015).

reciting passages from memory to my poor mother in order to get that checked off my to-do list. As much as I sometimes resented having to do that routine, I really appreciate it today.

Some 35+ years later, I can still call to mind many passages. I could be doing more today with this discipline. It would benefit me tomorrow by giving me the promises of God to hold on to. Tuck away the truth for use later. Inscribe it on the mind. Make it stick!

The key here is repetition.

We fill our minds with so many things. Why not the life-giving, Spirit-empowering word of God? In an age in which the opinions of men dominate our mental landscape, we need to make the extra effort to hold on to God's truth. It would be of great benefit for us as Christian leaders to memorize Scripture. If you have never tried memorizing Scripture, here are a few to get you started:

- Romans 5:8
- 1 John 1:1
- John 3:16-17
- John 1:14
- Isaiah 43:1-3a (if you are up for the challenge of a longer Section – this is one of my favorites!)

Meditate

Add to this a steady regimen of guided meditation, and you can train your mind to think on these things.

And now, dear brothers and sisters, one final thing. Fix your thoughts on what is true, and honorable, and right, and pure, and lovely, and admirable. Think about things that are excellent and worthy of praise (New Living Translation, Philippians 4:8).

Pay attention to breathing. Pay attention to where the body holds tension. Scan the body thoroughly and quietly. Legs, back, neck, jaw, feet, hands, arms, wrists, shoulders, even face. Observe the condition of your body and to what is happening in your mind. Pay attention to it. Don't try to control it. Let it go and learn to redirect back. Allow breath to enter and exit. Healthy rhythms. Deep breathing versus shallow. Clear, bright light…filling the body, and with each out breath, tension and worries carried away and removed with each exhalation. In and out. Commit to this practice just a few minutes each day and you will see benefit soon.

The key here is rest.

Don't try to do anything with what you are receiving at first. Simply hold it. Embrace it. Take it in.

Breathe and Receive.

Rest in the moment, in the present, and become fully alive with Christ.

Enjoy breathing.

Relaxed, but attentive posture. Upright, yet not tense. Pay attention.

Breathing has been shown to help with anxiety, insomnia, restlessness, focus, pain, and a host of other ailments that affect our health and wellness. We are complete, whole beings. Our spirituality is not separated from our physical, emotional selves.

This brief introduction to guided meditation is not in any way a comprehensive, or even expert discourse.

It would be of great benefit for us as Christian leaders to meditate.

Here are a few of the resources I like to use to help guide my meditation practice.

- A Christian Meditation Podcast[5]
- Pray as You Go[6]
- HeadSpace App[7]

Marinate, memorize, and meditate. Spend time. Repeat Scripture until it sticks. And meditate.

---

5 *A Christian Meditation Podcast,* http://christianmeditationpodcast.libsyn.com/
6 *Pray as You Go,* https://www.pray-as-you-go.org/home/
7 *HeadSpace App,* https://www.headspace.com/headspace-meditation-app

TRY THIS

Which one of the three M's do you want to try?

Marinate   *Memorize*   *Meditate*

Pick one and try it for a week. What did you discover? Was it easier or more difficult than you thought? If you liked it, try it again for another week. Or, try something different.

Tell a friend about one of the exercises or resources and have them try it and then get together and talk about the difference it made.

LESSON 4

I Wasn't Born with a Self-Concept

There are certain characteristics I was born with, that I have in my DNA. And there are many traits that I have acquired through the unique experiences in my journey. Among these is the opinion I hold about myself. It has been developing throughout my life.

This is good news. It means that I can re-form it. Not everything I subconsciously hold to be true about my identity, self-worth, value, is true. Plagued by many negative and self-defeating thoughts about myself, I can train my mind to BELIEVE the truth. And, here is the truth: that training comes by deliberately and consistently taking in the identity-shaping words of my Creator!

What has helped shape my identity to this point?

Culture, family, circumstances (good and bad), words spoken to me or about me, replayed narratives that are on a never-ending loop, expectations of others, traditions, denominational heritage, education, diagnoses, all mixed together with God's Word sprinkled in.

Do you see anything wrong with this picture? Sprinkling isn't enough. **Only** God has the full and true understanding of who I am. Therefore, I must seek Him to have an accurate and true view of who I am! I do not get some blessing from God in discounting myself. Neither do I get an accurate understanding of me without Him. Sprinkling isn't enough.

Perhaps you guard against the kinds of opinions that poison our own self-image. But it's more likely that you, like so many of us, have listened closer to criticism than to praise and have given others' damaging views of yourself a fixed position in your psyche. Many dreamers have. This reality can be one of the biggest dream wreckers. If I feel I am incapable, that I have nothing to offer, what happens when God puts a God-sized dream in my heart? I will need to wrestle with that dream as it comes up against my self-image.

Whether or not I get this makes no difference in reality. I am who **God** says I am! I am who **God** has created me to be! Period.

I can think and even believe the opposite, but my thinking or believing does not influence the truth. This is such a comfort for me. The reality of who I am is not actually impacted or changed by what I think. Truth is truth.

There has often been a huge disconnect for me. It's more of a tension of apparent opposites, and it shows up like this: I am a sinner in need of God's saving. Sinner, guilty, AND a child of God, divine heir of the Kingdom of Heaven WITH Christ on account of Christ. In my tradition there is so much emphasis on the former that the latter gets missed. *I* think I've missed that part.

Please don't misunderstand me. I've always **believed** that I am an heir to ALL of God's Kingdom enterprise. I've known it.... intellectually. However, I rarely embrace it, internalize it, adopt it into my psyche. I have not always lived my days or made decisions through that filter.

It is not that we should adopt one or the other, sinner or child of God. Or even one over the other. Both are true. The fullness of the Gospel is found when we plant both of these in our self-concept. For, God has said so. Clearly and consistently.

Thanks for forgiving me, Jesus. I sure am rotten, a blind beggar, lost without you. Yes, ALL TRUE because God has said so. Yet, incomplete. He also says this about me:

> "God saved you by his grace when you believed. And you can't take credit for this; it is a gift from God. Salvation is not a reward for the good things we have done, so none of us can boast about it. For we are God's masterpieces. He has created us anew in Christ Jesus, so we can do the good things he planned for us long ago."
>
> —New Living Translation, Ephesians 2:8-10

> "See how very much our Father loves us, for he calls us his children, and that is what we are! But the people who belong to this world don't recognize that we are God's children because they don't know him."
>
> —1 John 3:1

"So we have not stopped praying for you since we first heard about you. We ask God to give you complete knowledge of his will and to give you spiritual wisdom and understanding. Then the way you live will always honor and please the Lord, and your lives will produce every kind of good fruit. All the while, you will grow as you learn to know God better and better.

We also pray that you will be strengthened with all his glorious power so you will have all the endurance and patience you need. May you be filled with joy, always thanking the Father. He has enabled you to share in the inheritance that belongs to his people, who live in the light. For he has rescued us from the kingdom of darkness and transferred us into the Kingdom of his dear Son, who purchased our freedom and forgave our sins."

—Colossians 1:9-14

There's plenty more where those came from!

A self-defeating view of myself does not come from God. An incomplete view of one's self is insufficient for dreamers. Disagreeing with God will not be helpful for us. We need His Word concerning our identity as much as we need His word for the direction of our lives.

I have learned that my personality leans toward emphasizing a certain aspect of God's truth. I am a sinner, flawed, imperfect, needing forgiveness, needing work, etc. This lines up with me being a Type 4 on the Enneagram. (The Enneagram is an ancient personality typing system based on 9 personality types. Those 9 types are represented by numbers. For more information on the Enneagram, see *Appendix, p. 319.*) The danger with filtering God's truth through my personality type is that it gives me an incomplete view of myself. And, therefore, it also gives me an incomplete view of God. This is why I need to constantly allow space for His Word. I must listen to His voice speak to me about me.

TRY THIS

Where have you consistently disagreed with God?

As I listen to God, read His Word, are there things He tells me that are not lining up with what I believe to be true?

So what do I do in those moments, make my understanding subject to God's or make His truth subject to mine?

Or is the problem that I don't really even know what God thinks?

LESSON 5

Following Jesus Will Impact Every Aspect of Your Life, Not Just the "Spiritual" Part

There is no "spiritual part" of you. You are a whole person. And, as a whole person you are spiritual, physical, mental, emotional, intellectual, and relational. God has redeemed ALL of you in Jesus. There is no part of you that is untouched by His presence, His provision, His power.

Jesus cares about every aspect of your life. He cares about your waking life. He cares about your sleep. He cares that you are productive. He desires you to be free from the emotions that control you. He can help you with the management of your finances. He wants you to live in healthy, honest, and supportive friendships. He can help you learn how to have tough, but necessary conversations that yield harmony. He wants your business to thrive and be a blessing to others. He can do something about the long-held thought patterns that are keeping you stuck. He wants to see you using your gifts, time, and talents to benefit others.

Where are you compartmentalizing your life? What "part" of the whole have you been keeping from His influence? Seriously, right now is there some part of your life that you think might be too small, too messy, too embarrassing to open up and let Jesus influence? What is it? It might help to speak it out loud. Better yet, write it down. Acknowledge your need for help. Ask for input. Bring it out into the light of truth: "I have come that they might have life to the full" (New International Version, John 10:10). "Then you will know the truth, and the truth will set you free" John 8:32. -Jesus

He already knows ALL of it, every small detail. He created you. He knows you. He loves you. He is for you. Acknowledging it, making it public, bringing that hidden part out into the light helps you see it, and connect it to the whole of your life.

So, what's the hesitation? Why do we resist giving our Creator, Savior, Sustainer the pleasure of leading us? Why do we resist OUR own pleasure? Why do we resist the dream He sparks? I have discovered three culprits:

1) False Belief

Our understanding of God is limited. It is influenced by our finite experience. The result is a limited view of ourselves. We are also guilty of overemphasizing one part of God's character while minimizing other parts. And so we miss accessing a gift that is available to us right now, not waiting for us some day. We know that Jesus came to save us from our sin and provide the gift of heaven after we die, but all too often we forget about what Jesus offers us in the life we're living now. Think about it. If He is only our ticket to heaven and not also Lord of our day-to-day lives, what do we miss? Is He there only to bail us out? On the flip side, if He is our Model only and not our

Savior, how will that affect us? Is He simply a guru? We must grapple with these questions, which may be painful as they cast a spotlight on our limitations. We must re-align our understanding of He who sparks and rekindles dreams.

2) Fear

Fear of losing control. Fear of Him asking us to do something that we really don't want to do, or that we think we are incapable of doing. Fear that we will lose what we have. Fear of peoples' judgement. Fear of rejection.

There are plenty of stories in the Bible that show us how terrifying His call can be, right? Noah, Abraham. Isaiah, Jeremiah, Moses, Jonah, Paul, Peter, even Jesus! Shoot! Is there ever an instruction from the Lord to His chosen servants that doesn't come at some incredible cost or unbelievable discomfort!

examples

3) Fascination

With the bells and whistles of the world. With the voices counseling us from the world. With the thought of being our own boss. With the promises of power, privilege, position.

TRY THIS

Which one of the three culprits listed is causing you to resist the dream your Creator has sparked within you?

1. False Belief
2. Fear
3. Fascination

After you identify which one you struggle with most, reflect on what it would take to get past the struggle? Who could you talk to? Brainstorm ideas to overcome the culprit. Look at the list. Which idea from your brainstorm list are you willing to act on first? Who can help hold you accountable?

Personal Clarity Includes a General and Specific Calling

It is imperative that you follow your own dream. Trying to fit into someone else's mold robs the world of your unique contribution. The more clear you are about who you are, the less likely it is that you will get trapped by others' expectations.

God did not clone you. He created you as one of a kind. He is a Master Creator. And you are His masterpiece.

He must have a very good reason for creating such diversity in the human race. Consider the beauty and magnificent collection of unique individuals he has scattered throughout the earth. Pull together every single human being throughout history and yet to come and they would only begin to scratch the surface of the breadth and depth of His character. The countless expressions of humanity reflect His redemptive love, but as myriad as they are, they cannot reflect all of it.

Dreams have a general and specific nature to them, which makes sense because they spring from the hearts of individuals who have general and specific callings.

> *General calling*
> to spread God's redemptive love.
>
> *Specific Calling*
> the individually unique way that the general calling
> gets lived out in one's life.

General Calling

A general calling without a specific calling leads to duty and obligation.

It does so because it takes your unique contribution out of the equation. It leaves out creativity, perspective, and design. If you were not allowed to participate using your own uncommon perspective and extraordinary input, you would not be a part of your own story. You would only be providing manpower, an extra set of hands. That sounds almost barbaric. It certainly would be drudgery.

Part of what enriches any situation is the one-of-a-kind contribution of each participant. The flavor, beauty, richness, depth, and quality that an individual adds are all reflections of the diversity of God's gifts. A project only becomes whole when people play their particular part by putting to use their specialties.

Without diversity of expression, we get monotony.

Specific Calling

A specific calling without a general calling leads to barrenness.

Living for yourself without partnership is self-serving and powerless. Imagine a lifetime defined by a series of selfies. Where is the greater significance? Narcissism is so isolating. Certainly, it is no joint effort. Esprit de corps, synergy, working together... this is what we get (to enjoy!) when we combine gifts. We can accomplish more together than we can alone. Capacity expands when we unite for a great cause.

Some of my most exciting and fulfilling moments have come when I played on a team. On the basketball court, in the office, in Sunday's service, in the Boardroom, at the design table. Whether it has been playing a game, writing curriculum, leading worship, facilitating a group, drawing the best out of a roomful of leaders, or making music in the band, joining together can be exhilarating. Our efforts will find their true value in their addition to the whole.

We will never find a greater unifying mission than the one our Savior has shared with us. So why not play our part?

Individualistic focus is impotent.

Conceit, self-absorption, isolated, egotism waste our gifts and stunt our growth.

In my work with churches I see the dynamics of copycatting at every turn. The work I do is to help churches and ministry organizations identify and then become who they were uniquely designed to be. There is a lack of understanding that each local organization is set apart from every other in the community. From this comes competition instead of cooperation, comparison instead of collaboration. Such a lack of understanding renders the mission impotent.

It's the same for people.

Personal clarity on the two fronts of general calling and specific calling will be a tremendous asset for you as you seek to live a fruitful and productive life.

Your **general calling** answers the question *what?*

Determined by divine directives and divine gifting matched up with an evident, and common human need, your general calling adds mission.

Your **specific calling** answers the question *how?*

Determined by unique interests, talents, opportunities, and perspectives, your specific calling adds diversity.

Where these intersect there is great freedom, power, and fruitfulness.

TRY THIS

Consider this quote from American writer, preacher, and theologian, Frederick Buechner:

"The place where God calls you to is the place where your deep gladness and the world's deep hunger coincide." [8]

Draw a Venn diagram with two overlapping circles. In one of the circles write out all the things you notice right now in the world that trouble you. In the other circle write out all of the things you love to do, the activities that give you great joy. In the overlapped section of the two circles attempt to make some connections. Where does the world's deep hunger connect with your giftedness?

What do you notice here?

---

8 Frederick Buechner, *Wishful Thinking: A Theological ABC*, (San Francisco: HarperOne, 1973), 95.

LESSON 7

But This I Call to Mind, and, Therefore, I Have Hope

Many people believe that dreaming is only for others. For them, they think, there is little chance that a dream can be sparked. Any flicker of thought, any small dream spark would be quickly snuffed out by a cold draft of reality. So why even bother?

That will never work. Who am I kidding? I don't have time for this. Dreaming is for people who have cash to burn. I have responsibilities. Responsibilities trump dreams.

YOUR dream must live!

For the dream to be given a chance to live you need hope.

With dreams there is a lack of certainty. At first, the dream exists solely in the imagination. It needs space to develop, to be considered. Don't kill it before it has a chance to enter the world. Most dreams do not die due to failure. They die of our fear of failure before they are ever launched.

In order for our dreams to be sparked we will need persistent hope.

In the middle of the uncertainty, a light can break through. Right in the midst of the debilitating lies, renewal begins. Hope needs to keep doubt and fear in check so you can move forward.

How do we do this so that our dreams are not hijacked? By making a simple declaration. By making a deliberate choice and making it persistently.

> But this I call to mind, and therefore I have hope: (English Standard Version, Lamentations 3:21).

A different translation interprets the text this way:

> Yet I still dare to hope when I remember this: (New Living Translation, Lamentations 3:21).

Dare to hope. Dare to dream. Dream big. In spite of the realities that are getting in the way of the pursuit of that dream. This is perhaps the biggest lesson in dreaming big. Because the dream, your dream, sometimes seems so big, so daunting it is critical to *call to mind*, to *remember*. What?

The familiar refrain follows.

> The steadfast love of the LORD never ceases; his mercies never come to an end; they are new every morning; great is your faithfulness (English Standard Version, Lamentations 3:22-23).

The refrain interrupts with hope. But, only if verse 21 is executed.

"Call to mind"..."remember this" The original language (Hebrew) literally means to turn back, or return to. This knowledge is already there. It has already been given and received. It is a truth that remains because it never left. Even in the darkness, pain, and toil described in verses 1-20, He who restores hope is right there. He can be accessed.

But how?

Before I answer that, let me ask another question. How is it that the painful moments and debilitating realities stay with you? How do you allow those dark interludes to linger? Is there anything to learn here? Can we apply the same choice, the same attention to what follows the colon in verse 21?

If you can dwell in the darkest place, can you not also choose to dwell in the promises that produce hope and light?

A friend recently said to me, "I choose joy." I love that. But how?

By remembering, calling to mind, returning back to...(wait for it)... God. By remembering to remember. Or you might say by recalling to recall.

> The steadfast love of the LORD never ceases; his mercies never come to an end; they are new every morning; great is your faithfulness (English Standard Version, Lamentations 3:22-23).

Think on **Him**. Consider **Him**. Speak **His** promises.

Linger on each phrase. *The steadfast love of the LORD never ceases*

What do you notice? What impresses you about this? How does this truth play out in your life? Where do you need the Lord's steadfast love today? *his mercies never come to an end* What is *mercy?* Where do you need it today? *Never come to an end,* under any circumstance.

What circumstance today is afflicting you? What happens to the affliction when you apply the *never? they are new every morning* What is new? What does this truth mean for you? Ponder it. Stay here awhile. Don't rush past. *great is your faithfulness.* What is faithfulness? How would you describe it? Put *great is your faithfulness* into your own words. Place it right in the middle of today. How does this change things? How does this impact your day, even if the circumstances don't change? And so it goes; the turning back, the calling to mind, the remembering. Daily, sometimes even more frequently. Consider the promises of God. Linger there. Remember them. Memorize them. Focus on them. Then, and only then, will the life-gift called hope begin to pierce the darkness and dare to shine through, redirecting you time and again to the source of your dream, the reason for it, and the certainty within it.

DREAM
CIRCLE

TRY THIS

Pick a promise of God from His Word. Like Lamentations 3:22, for example. And get creative on how you can return to it each day.

- Begin your day lingering on each phrase.
- Use some of the questions in this section.
- Pick your own questions.
- Write it out 5 times in your journal.
- Memorize it.
- Carry it with you like a flash card.
- Pull it out during a break, at lunch.
- Post it on your bathroom mirror.
- Ask a friend to text it to you every day this week at 1 p.m.
- Let it be the first thing you consider each morning, and the last thing you look at before you fall asleep.

LESSON 8

Neighbors Make Great Friends

For ministry professionals one of the greatest unexplored treasures is friendship.

In fact, some of us were taught that we are not supposed to have friends within the church. The thought goes something like this "You can't provide the appropriate pastoral care if you have lost your objectivity in friendship." This frequently leaves professional church workers lonely and unfulfilled.

A true friendship is rare. Any google search for "pastors and loneliness" or "church worker and loneliness" will produce a minefield of explosive truth. Here's one insightful observation, which starts: "It's ironic that pastors, who talk the most about the need for community, experience it the least."[9] Or this from a group called ExPastor that has made it their mission to help those who are struggling: "70% do not have someone they consider a close friend and 40% report serious conflict with a parishioner at least once a

---

9 Mark Brouwer, *Where Can Pastors Find Real Friends,* (Christianity Today CT Pastors), http://www.christianitytoday.com/pastors/2014/march-online-only/friendless-pastor.html.

month."[10] As I write this first draft this morning, this post has 28,187 shares. Sobering.

It's the cost of our calling. So we are told. At the Seminary I was taught that pastors should not have friends within the church. I was also taught that my role was primarily to take care of the church and those already within the walls of the sanctuary. This combination, no friends + stay in the church = loneliness. How could it not lead to loneliness?

If our calling includes helping people on their spiritual journey, with their life in Jesus, and if a life in Jesus includes vulnerable and true friendship, then what we've been taught simply does not add up. It's not working. And, fundamentally, it hinders us as witnesses to Jesus at home, in our neighborhoods, and abroad.

In the church we are a group that simply does not know how to nurture friendships. Ouch!

It is common for pastors when they retire from their "calling" to have a very difficult time in relationships. No wonder. They have rarely experienced friendship. And because a vast majority of pastors grew up in the church, they have never been discipled in a Christ-centered friendship.

If this resonates with you, what can you do?

May I make three suggestions?

---

10 Bo Lane, *Why Do So Many Pastors Leave the Ministry? The Facts Will Shock You,* (Expastors), http://www.expastors.com/why-do-so-many-pastors-leave-the-ministry-the-facts-will-shock-you/.

1. Pray fervently for God to show you someone that can be your friend. Then follow His lead and risk vulnerability. If you want a friend, then be approachable or "friendable." Enjoy that friendship.
2. Explore friendship in your neighborhood. No converting. Just be a friend. I think you might find it refreshing.
3. Own your life. Don't simply complain that you don't have friends. Make an effort to be a friend. Make a decision to nurture friendship. No one will do this for you. The risk of disappointment is worth it in the end. Don't get to the end of your ministry, whether that be five years, or 50 years, and discover that you have no friends.

Life is more fulfilling with friendship.

#2 was a great discovery for me over the past decade. The gift of friendship in my neighborhood was one of the blessings during the six-month sabbatical I took from the local church that surprised me. Forcing yourself to get involved in new areas and with new people can open doors that you never anticipated opening.

I'll never forget that first Wednesday in December at the beginning of the sabbatical. Instead of going to church for our midweek Advent worship experience I met with some of the men from my neighborhood at a local establishment. Props to the Hop Haus in Verona, WI! I was so energized by our conversation. I had discovered that I had more in common with these brothers than I had anticipated. I came home and said to Amy, "That was the best Advent worship I have ever experienced!" This wasn't a theological statement, of course. It was a relationship statement. Change is good.

Making friends almost by definition brings new changes into your life.

We have been blessed with some great friendships within the church. For this I am extremely thankful. Lifelong friendships have endured. We are also discovering that neighbors make great friends too.

TRY THIS

Try out the 3 suggestions that were listed.

1. Pray fervently for God to show you who you can be friends with.
2. Explore friendships in your neighborhood. Just enjoy them.
3. Own your life. Be intentional about nurturing your friendships. Take time with those relationships.

The Search for the Great Three: Love, Peace, Joy

Love, Peace, Joy. Just about everyone's dream includes them.

There is so much searching for these today. The alarming increase of mass shootings, unethical and unprofessional leadership, busyness and overextension is underscoring our desperate need for love, peace, and joy. The Great Three are like sand slipping through our fingers. Pursuing the Great Three is like chasing after the wind. They are definable yet they seem to be beyond our reach. So, we live our lives without them. They may be up there on the mantle, adorning our living space as a decoration, but they are not employed in our daily lives. They have not become incorporated into our daily rhythms. And because we worship the idea, but fail to bring it into our reality, we continue to settle for less. They remain outside of our existence. We struggle to touch them, discern them, and experience them.

We also pray that you will be strengthened with all his glorious power so you will have all the endurance and patience you need. May you be filled with joy, always thanking the Father. He has enabled you to share in the inheritance that belongs to his people, who live in the light. For he has rescued us from the kingdom of darkness and transferred us into the Kingdom of his dear Son, who purchased our freedom and forgave our sins (New Living Translation, Colossians 1:11-14).

I encourage you to define what seems to be indefinable. Any attempt to do so will lead to a description. Love is like... Go ahead. Love, peace, joy. Describe them. Our descriptions may serve as dramatic revelations of our personal experience. These ideas can also become ideals. They escape our reality and dwell somewhere in the realm of the unapproachable, unable of being experienced by limited, mortal creatures like you and me. This is why we hear people speak about them as if they are just out of reach. "I want some peace." "I long for love." "I wish I could shake this feeling and finally experience some joy." The Great Three are just beyond our grasp.

This is true because we search for them away from their source.

As long as we do this, we will continue to search. In vain. Only God makes the invisible visible, intangible tangible, indiscernible brilliantly real. God made and is making the Great Three available! What? Really? Seriously? For me? YES!! God is not veiled! He is love. He is joy. He is peace. The Great Three cannot be defined or experienced apart from Him. He does not simply produce the Great Three. He *is* the Great Three.

How is this possible? Jesus. God has chosen to place the Great Three in Christ. God has chosen to place all His fullness in Christ and deliver them to humans in the flesh!

> "And the Word became flesh and made His dwelling among us. We have seen His glory" (John 1:14).

All the fullness of God in Jesus. All the fullness of the Great Three in Jesus.

As I consider the truth of all that is written here, here's what I'm thinking I can do about it. Call them takeaways, if you wish.

Pursue Jesus.

Praise God more. Ask for stuff less.

Position yourself to observe.

TRY THIS

Pursue Jesus. Chase after Him with the same vigor you pursue career, athletic success, grades, human companionship, ministry success. Because love, joy, and peace are not found in those pursuits apart from Him! They can only be found in those pursuits alongside of Him.

Praise God more. Ask for stuff less. Stop asking for the Great Three. Act "as if" they are already yours. Instead of asking for them and searching for them, receive them. Realign your prayers from "Dear Lord, give me the Great Three." to "Author and Provider of the Great Three, I praise You for who YOU ARE. You are Love. You are Peace. You are Joy. Walk with me today. And, as you do, open my eyes to see the Great Three in you."

Position yourself to observe. Create some much-needed space in your day. At the outset. In the middle. At the end. To consider Him. To remember Him.

- Envision it at the outset.
- Stop the runaway train in the middle and realign.
- And review it at the end. Rinse and repeat.

LESSON 10

Unsettled Leaders Need a Spark

When I use the term, leader, I am referring to every follower. A leader is first and foremost a follower. We are leaders under the commission of Jesus. HE is our leader. Anyone who follows Jesus is a leader. He has appointed us in our baptism to go and make disciples.

And leaders are in desperate need of sparks! An encouraging word. An idea. A nudge. Permission.

It only takes a spark to get a fire going.

As I work with Christian leaders, both those with official titles and those who are faithful in their following without official titles, I am reminded constantly that one of the greatest things that is needed is encouragement, which I am fortunate to be able to provide. Often encouragement comes in the form of simply giving permission to try. When I say "try," I mean to attempt whatever God has prompted you to go and do without reservation, without any angst about the outcome. The original title of this book was "Permission Granted!" But there were already dozens of books by that title, a testament to all the fear in our ranks!

Fear unchallenged over time leaves one feeling unsettled. It's difficult to dream when we are anxious, agitated, or restless. A state of fearfulness keeps us stuck. And, when we're stuck we can't dream.

If you are feeling unsettled right now, be encouraged. There is a way out. Sit down for a little bit. Consider some of the sources of new ideas that are right in front of you. I call them "sparks."

Sparks

Brainstorm

Stop evaluating as you dream. Turn down your critical faculties for a moment. The goal of brainstorming is to get as many ideas down on the page as you can. In this process it is important to wait through silence and push through when you think you have exhausted your ideas. It is usually when we think we have run dry that a gold nugget reveals itself.

Here are a few questions that may get those synapses firing again:

- What do you want to try that you have already talked yourself out of?
- If you had absolutely nothing to lose, what would you try?
- What have you wanted to attempt in the past, but have always resisted?
- If these questions haven't sparked what you were hoping for, press on with these questions:
- What's the craziest idea you can think of?
- What would a 5 year old do in this situation?

Pick one of your favorite leaders and ask yourself what they would do.

If I were _____ in this situation, I would

_____.

Read, Read, Read

It really doesn't matter what. Read business books, novels, short works, long ones, fiction, inspirational non-fiction. Just read. Reading will stimulate your thinking and inspire your dreaming. It will spark ideas and enliven your thoughts.

Write, Write, Write

Look for Interesting Combinations of Ideas

Sometimes the best ideas are a combination of a couple of different approaches. With some mixing and tweaking, you may discover a "third option" that really works for you. For example, recently I was trying to get a couple of friends to read the Bible with me. We talked about doing this for months, but could not land on a date or time that worked for all of us. Our calendars were simply too full. We couldn't find time to meet. Everyone was getting frustrated and about to give up trying. Talking about this challenge with another supportive friend, the question was asked, "What if you didn't have to be physically present in the same room as you read together?" Insert slap to the forehead. Duh. It unlocked an approach I hadn't considered. We now read together using Google Hangouts after their kids are in bed. Instead of wrangling over dates and times, we are doing what we set out to do.

Apply Scripture

As you read the Bible, stop and ask, does what I am reading today have anything to say about my current unsettledness? What is God's Word prompting me to do in response? How can I remember this scripture and reflect on it in the coming days?

Warning: it is easy for a spark to get snuffed out. Please be careful with your spark. Don't share it too soon. Only with proper kindling, will it turn into a fire.

TRY THIS

Need a spark? Schedule a Brainstorm session with a supportive friend. Ask the questions listed in the lesson and write down your responses.

Here are a few more questions to ask as you brainstorm.

What ideas have gripped you and won't let go? These are the ideas that, perhaps in spite of your resistance, you may need to come to terms with in order to make real progress.

What is an idea that has inspired you? Perhaps with your own particular spin on it, you could make it unique.

What hobby of yours calls out for more attention? Could you leverage it for good? Something that benefits others?

Which idea on the brainstorm list gives you the most energy or excitement? Which one are you going to act on?

LESSON 11

The Enemy of My Soul
Does Not Want Me to Dream

Wait. What? There is an enemy of my soul?

Yep. He's real. He's smart. He's tricky. And he desires nothing more than your complete destruction. He's intent on dragging you relentlessly into the pit. Jesus said that this enemy's objective is to "steal, kill, and destroy" (John 10:10). Nice.

His attack comes in two waves. In the first, he will do anything he can to keep you from dreaming. Jesus commissions you to dream. He prompts you to dream without fear. Satan, the king of fear, prohibits you from dreaming. The dreams of Jesus-followers make him shutter! So, he will not shy away from the challenge to disrupt and destroy your dream before it starts.

Be prepared for the second wave. If you have weathered the storm and dreamed a God-inspired dream, the enemy will marshal his forces to do anything he can to keep you from pursuing that dream. He will erect all kinds of barriers. He is a master-strategist and will use all of his tricks.

Here are five of his faves. Call them the dirty D's of the devil.

1.   Discouragement: He induces you to focus on your difficulties rather than on God.
2.   Doubt: He compels you to lose faith in God's Word and His goodness.
3.   Distraction: He diverts your attention from the great to the good. *Good* doesn't sound so bad, you might be thinking. And that's the point. How often are we *settling* when we could be *excelling*?
4.   Defeat: He presses you to fixate on your failure so you want to quit trying.
5.   Delay: He tempts you to put off doing something so that it never gets done.[11]

Here is the good news. The enemy is limited. He is not all-powerful. God is. Once the enemy's tactics are identified, their effect weakens, and they can be overcome. He might be *a* master-strategist. But, God is *THE* MASTER-STRATEGIST. The enemy has tricks. God has truth.

The next time you are inspired by God to dream a better future, and you start to have reservations, REMEMBER where the dream originated, by whose powers of creation and fulfillment it emerged, in whose foundry it was forged and minted. Renounce the enemy. Put him in his place. Rebuke him. Say it out loud. At your baptism, there was a declaration made: "I renounce the devil, all his works, and all his ways." That was more than just some mythical statement

---

11 Adapted from the *Life Application Bible*, New Living Translation, (Wheaton: Tyndale House, 2004), 11.

uttered ritualistically at a religious ceremony. That is the vocabulary of one who follows Jesus. It is also part of what Martin Luther was talking about when he encouraged Jesus followers to "remember their baptism daily."

Remember who you are in Christ. Remember Christ's position in your life. Remember also to renounce the enemy. Keep pushing him out of your business.

Here are a few tricks of your own. Consider these countermoves to the enemy's tactics. Use them relentlessly.

Speak Truth

Out loud. On paper. Challenge your thoughts. Challenge your feelings. With truth. Your enemy is the father of lies. Your God is Truth!

Execute Your System

Establish your rhythm. See Part 2: Lesson 2. Practice. Experiment. Adjust. Stick to it. Stack habit on habit.

Speed Forward

Start immediately. Don't look back.

TRY THIS

Pick the 1 or 2 D's that are particularly challenging you at the moment.

Ask yourself: How specifically is the enemy using this trick to thwart my dreams?

Identify your NEXT STEP in addressing this trick of the enemy's and take THAT STEP!

Look up Scripture that speaks to your soul and encourages you in the midst of this battle.

Here are some suggestions.

- Discouragement: Joshua 1:9, Galatians 6:9
- Doubt: Mark 9:24, Proverbs 3:5-6
- Distraction: Hebrews 12:1-3
- Defeat: Habakkuk 3:17-19, Romans 5:3-5
- Delay: Philippians 3:14

What other verses can you find that remind you of the victory that is yours?

Passion Is the Secret Ingredient

Everybody loves to participate in something where the people are excited about what they are doing.

I'm not a tequila drinker, but meeting Juan in Indianapolis and hearing his story about being a part of generations of tequila makers in Mexico got my attention. Feeling his excitement as he described the process and all the different kinds of tequilas was a lot of fun!

Talking at length to Tony at Nordstrom's share his passion for fashion and service helped me understand the appeal of a job I'd never paid much attention to.

Recently, in a conversation with a leader at *the Church* we discovered that their service at church had become a bit of a drag. They were burdened by it. They had been doing it for a long time, and they needed a change of scenery. By considering the simple question, "what would you like to do?," they were set free to make a change.

Life is too short to limit our focus to obligation.

Being around people who are excited and fulfilled about what they do is contagious. You want to hear more. You're intrigued. You're drawn in.

Movements that have passion as a real foundational characteristic cannot be stopped.

What have you been wanting to try, but haven't? Stop waiting and try it!

In terms of following Jesus, what are you intrigued about? Where are you excited to jump in? What gets your heart beating more quickly?

Let's look at this from another angle. Are there Jesus followers whom you observe having fun, enjoying what they are doing? Who are the Juans or Tonys who could share what they are doing and why they love it so much? Sit with them. Take them to lunch. Listen to their story. Maybe their passion will rub off on you.

My wife, Amy, went to Ethiopia for seven consecutive years. The first year ignited six more. She couldn't miss it. She has tried to get me to join her every single year. Going to Ethiopia every February gave her a boost of energy and passion!

The stories of the Ethiopian Christians in the Ethiopian Evangelical Church Mekane Yesus (EECMY) are so inspiring. I love hearing about their passion, dedication, and joy. Recently at a Board meeting for an organization I'm a part of, we brought in a young man from Ethiopia. As he shared his passion for Jesus and multiplying missional leaders in his homeland so they could reach the entire African continent, I was moved to tears. He then shared how his church body in Ethiopia has a strategy to send missionaries to America. He promised that the West would be impacted by the Jesus followers in Africa.

I have had similar experiences. When I was in India I wanted to bring back home the Christians I met there and introduce them to the congregation I serve! If there was some way they could simply meet with our people, maybe some of that passion would go viral, as one would say in today's parlance.

I have a friendship with two servants of Jesus who live in Nepal. They work tirelessly throughout the country loving people and telling them about Jesus. They ride scooters for days through rugged terrain delivering boxes of Bibles. I see pictures of them housing and feeding street children. Giving warm blankets to cold villagers. Marching with other Christians down the streets of Kathmandu as police look on. Such boldness. Such faith.

Where does that passion come from?

For them Jesus is real. He is not a philosophy. He is not a theological ideology. He is not systematic discourse. He is the living Savior who lived, died, and lives! He is the Good News for our struggling planet. He is the answer. For every need, for every situation, He lives.

And, here's the thing that I think separates those who are on fire from those who are lukewarm: there is an awe in their understanding that Jesus has invited them to be full participants in the Father's mission. It's like, "Man, I can't believe I get to do this. Why would God let me play? This is so cool."

How do we capture this passionate spirituality in America? How do we heat up our lukewarmness and accept this white-hot reality?

American Christians are a lot like the Laodiceans in Revelation 3. Open up your Bible and follow along. Do you see the progression to white-hot passion?

Recognize Our Deep Need

This is hard for us, if not impossible. We say, "I am rich. I have everything I want. I don't need a thing!" And [we] don't realize that we are wretched and miserable and poor and blind and naked" (Revelation 3:17).

Rejoice in the Triumph That Proceeds from Such a Need!

"Those who are victorious will sit with me on my throne, just as I was victorious and sat with my Father on his throne" (Revelation 3:21).

Invest in Kingdom of Jesus Pursuits

"So I advise you to buy gold from me-gold that has been purified by fire. Then you will be rich. Also buy white garments from me so you will not be shamed by your nakedness, and ointment for your eyes so you will be able to see. I correct and discipline everyone I love. So be diligent and turn from your indifference" (New Living Translation, Revelation 3:18-19).

Your heart follows your investment. Your time, talent, and treasure are often the means God uses to engage your heart and fire up white-hot faith.

Hang Out with Jesus

"Look! I stand at the door and knock. If you hear my voice and open the door, I will come in, and we will share a meal together as friends" (New living Translation, Revelation 3:20).

Dreams are forged here. They become an unquenchable white-hot pursuit.

TRY THIS

"Let my soul be at rest again, for the Lord has been good to me. He has saved me from death, my eyes from tears, my feet from stumbling. And so I walk in the Lord's presence as I live here on earth."

—Psalm 116:7-9

What have you been wanting to try, but haven't yet?

LESSON 13

Find Those Who
Truly Support Your Dream

Not everyone will support your dream. It is critical that you learn to identify those who will.

Some things are hidden. And they will remain hidden. Not everything we see is the way things really are. And we don't see everything that is real.

Only God can see the human heart and truly know its condition. There are people who are close to you who influence your decisions, your thoughts, your contemplations in a way that is not helpful, honest, or healthy. They do this intentionally and unintentionally. It doesn't matter which. Julia Cameron calls them "Crazymakers" in her most excellent work, The Artist's Way.[12] Affected by fear, jealousy, their own dependency on others' opinions, they interfere with your pursuit.

I would like to clarify that we also don't want to turn away loved ones who are brave enough to tell us uncomfortable truths. Finding the

---

12 Julia Cameron, *The Artist's Way: A Spiritual Path to Higher Creativity*, (New York: Penguin Putnam, 1992, 2002), 44.

difference between a "crazy-maker" and a tough-love friend, whom we dismiss out of defensiveness is difficult, no doubt.

Here are a few tips to help you distinguish one from the other. Pay attention to the moves of the person in question. Step back every once and awhile and observe their tactics. Consider this question Does this person want you to attain your goals or not?

Then ask yourself these more specific questions. Do they...

- listen or give advice?
- motivate or burden you with expectation?
- celebrate with you or find loopholes in your plan?
- empower you or distract you?
- repeat questions you have already answered?

Hint: You would probably be better served to surround yourself with people for whom you tick more of the former options to these questions than the latter.

How do you feel after you are with them? Is there a certain unease? Regain your identity. Reclaim your power. Re-engage your unique calling as a child of God by listening to Him! Spend more time with your Master, Creator, and Dream-maker than you do with them. Worry about His support, not theirs.

It is so crucial that pleasing others is not among our primary motivations to lead: You may think you are pleasing others, that they are "with" you, when in reality, they are not. The more energy you devote to pleasing others, the less likely it is that you will succeed: one, because you may become blind to their true feelings and, two, because people can be fickle and may take for granted those who take on a subservient role.

So, here's my advice: follow God's directive. Listen to Him. Keep your focus on what He has for you to do. Love people, but don't try to win their approval. In the end, it is simply not worth it. And, more importantly, it doesn't work.

Your job in life is to simply follow God. Live your life under His leadership. Learning to love people without basing your entire self-image on their opinion of you (something that is ultimately beyond your control) is one of THE keys to fulfilling your call and pursuing your God-given dream.

Recognizing and addressing the reality that we are often motivated by the approval of others will help us recover integrity, freedom, and power. Your greatest ally in this journey is God. He is with you. That is enough. People will come and go. There is an ebb and flow to their involvement in your life. Perhaps this all seems a bit austere. It is actually freeing because it unhooks us from people's approval and connects us with God who loves us and accepts us regardless of our performance. You have His approval before you take one step toward your dream!

Live out this truth and it puts those relationships with people in perspective and releases you to work with them, love them, and enjoy them with none of their expectations enslaving you.

TRY THIS

Awareness exercise: Take a moment and think about the list of people who are closest to you right now. By closest, in this case, I simply mean those with whom you spent most of your (free) time. They have your attention. Make a list of ten. Go through the five questions below and answer them honestly for each of those people.

- listen or give advice?
- motivate or burden you with expectation?
- celebrate with you, or find loopholes in your plan?
- empower you or distract you?
- repeat questions you have already answered?

LESSON 14

Vulnerability Is Difficult, but Essential

Recently, the idea that vulnerability is a weakness has been challenged.

Vulnerability is not a handicap or a liability. It is actually one of the truest measures of courage and strength.

Brene' Brown, clinical researcher at Rice University who has presented one of the most popular Ted Talks, defines vulnerability as "uncertainty, risk, and emotional exposure."[13] Let's go with that definition.

When was the last time you resisted uncertainty? You may have felt like you needed a sure plan before you asked anyone to join you. You measured the effectiveness of your leadership by executing the plan. When things got difficult because of the intrusion of the unexpected, you questioned your leadership competency.

When was the last time you resisted risk? You may have felt like the sure thing would be the only thing that you would dare to commit

---

13 Brene' Brown, *The Power of Vulnerability*, (TED Talk, Jan. 4, 2011), https://www.ted.com/talks/brene_brown_on_vulnerability?language=en.

to. You have come to fear and scorn the unfamiliar. "Too big a dream, it will never work anyway," you tell yourself. "It's not worth the risk."

When was the last time you covered up your weakness? You had to be the "strong one." You had to prove that you could do it by yourself. You had to fight for everything you got. If you had asked for help, you would have become dependent.

Are you afraid of uncertainty? Do you shy away from risk? Are you afraid to show weakness?

Embrace the surprises. Life promises them.

Embrace the experiment. Nothing moves forward without one.

Embrace your need. A community is formed through mutual needs.

Why is leading with vulnerability so important? Why is vulnerability actually critical for dreams to live?

1. Jesus led with vulnerability. Jesus is the model of leadership to which we aspire. "Greater love has no one than this, that someone lay down his life for his friends" (English Standard Version, John 15:13). If this kind of trust and vulnerability is good enough for the Leader of leaders, then it is good enough for me.
2. Allows us to depend on Jesus. When we rely on Jesus our weakness actually becomes the place where His strength takes over.
3. Keeps you from falling into pride. If the Divine has sparked your dream, then He owns it. Because He owns it, He

sustains it and He defends it. Embracing our place in this equation frees us to receive our role in the dream as a gift. And it keeps us from the pressure of human striving.

4. It is the key to forming deep relational connections. There are no relationships without mutual needs.

5. Vulnerability allows us to explore a reality outside of our got-to-get-right-all-the-time-to prove-my-worth adult headspace. It opens us up to see our limitations, but also to embrace our unique strengths. In other words, vulnerability empowers us to be unapologetically who we really are.

Disclaimer: let's be clear about what vulnerability really is. It entails risk, which can cost you greatly. These days, people throw around the term as if it were purely positive. Unfortunately, that's not the case.

Showing vulnerability isn't easy. There will be those in your life who will use your vulnerability against you. They will see it as a weakness and use those moments as opportunity to gain an advantage. At least, then you can refine your dream-supporter list.

Be prepared to have the intimate fears that you shared confidentially brought out in public. Expect a few in your inner circle to exploit the trust you placed in them, to push you down as they boost themselves up. Some may resent you for showing vulnerability and this resentment may compromise the friendship. Perhaps they were only riding the coattails of your success and jumped off at the first sign of what they perceived as failure. Don't be caught off guard or surprised by this phenomenon. If and when you experience these kinds of painful effects of vulnerability, remember that you are not alone in this experience. It's quite natural. These moments do not have to be dream killers.

Dreams always tap into our vulnerability. They are not for the faint of heart. Yet they take a vulnerable heart to get off the ground. Uncertainty, risk, and weakness (perceived and real) are basic ingredients of any dream. It's helpful to understand this reality.

Childhood was full of these ingredients. Tapping into our inner child is a key to overcoming fear and dreaming big. That's probably why one of my favorite brainstorming coaching questions to help people unlock a dream or get unstuck from their current situation is "What would a 5 year old do in this situation?" If you don't hold the same respect for the decision-making skills of a 5-year old, perhaps that's the point: to get outside of our adult headspace.

What WOULD a 5 year old do? Let yourself consider the question. Then experiment with the answer and act on it. Just see how it turns out. See how you feel acting on it.

Yes, there are dangers with dreams. They will expose you. And, that can bring disappointment, pain, and challenges.

Yet, the benefits and gains far outweigh the costs.

TRY THIS

Think about a time when you recently were hesitant to show your emotion? What was fueling your reluctance? What did you think you would lose if you let weakness show?

Let your guard down...

Think about what the motivation was for you in that moment.

Journal your thoughts.

LESSON 15

Waiting Is Hard

Some say it's the hardest part. Waiting. Ruminating about *what could be* when you are stuck in the *what is* can really suck the life out of you. Stop it then. Don't settle for the *what is*. You are going to have to confront what may initially seem a bit contradictory: 1) you can only live in the present, and 2) God has placed the future dream in your heart. Both are true. Embrace the tension. Because in that tension is the gold! The pursuit of the dream, a future achievement, is lived out in the present. As a friend summarized my book, "Fear is the problem; the dream the solution; execution our path forward."

Living in the present with hope and joy while you wait for something you truly long for is the hardest part. Can I make a broad-sweeping generalization to solve all of your current challenges in this area?

While you wait for your circumstances to change, change your circumstances.

Now, doesn't that make everything all better? Too abstract, you say? Ok. Try this. Start with what is right in front of you. What can you control? (Serenity Prayer) What you are waiting for will only come if you are faithful in the moments in front of you right now. The future is realized by the steps you take in the present.

Need something more specific and hands-on? Ok. Ok. Ok. Here are three concrete suggestions you might consider acting on right now to help you on your way.

Write out What You Are Waiting For

Utilizing your most creative, precise language, spell it out. Describe what you are waiting for and how you expect to feel when it arrives.

Use the Dream to Set Some Goals You Can Execute Right Now

Don't allow any adverse circumstances in the present be an excuse. Actively pursue the dream right now. Drop the excuses and relentlessly pursue the dream. As you look at what you wrote describing what you are waiting for, think about one or two things you could do today as a first step. This may be a more critical time than you realize. How can you make better use of this time? What's your next move?

Appreciate the Present

Your life is more about the journey than about the destination. See the value in what is right in front of you. You may miss something really important if all you are focused on is a destination way out beyond the horizon. I'm not saying you should never consider life beyond the horizon. Occasionally looking at your future can help you keep moving in that direction. It IS important to know where you are going. But, that destination is only going to be realized

IF you take the next step right in front of you. *Glance* beyond the horizon. *Gaze* at what lies right in front of you. The present is chalk full of experience, understanding and discovery that will deepen the reality of your future. God is not just a God who is out there beyond the horizon waiting for you to find Him. He is with you right now, even in the mundane wish-I-were-somewhere-else. He is Immanuel just as surely as He is Eternal Life. In fact, life in Jesus is an eternal relationship that begins right now, in the present! "Thy will be done on earth as it is in heaven," right?

Is it starting to sink in? As you begin to get some clarity on your dream, the pull to dismiss it will gather strength, unfortunately. It will seem more and more daunting when you focus on what you cannot control. You cannot control the future. You can only control your now. In fact, the future will more than likely diverge from the scenario you envisioned when your dream was first sparked. So, hold on, and enjoy the ride. Be a full participant right now by taking that first obvious step.

In response to a question on my Facebook page "If you have dreamed a dream, how do YOU not become overwhelmed with all that needs to be done in order to achieve it?" A friend responded, "Surrender." She went on to explain: God "takes it in dips and turns we wouldn't have wanted or expected and then does something incredible with it…." So, surrender the future to God.

Surrender by taking the next step.

TRY THIS

Take these three suggestions and execute them this week.

Write out what you are waiting for. Describe it using your most vivid language. Make it come alive. Once you have done this, go through your description and pull out the five most important points you want to remember. Bullet point them. Place the bullet points below your narrative.

Use your description to shape some goals. Based on this clear description of a destination you are waiting for, what are a couple of things you could do this week, today, right now? Think next step, not ultimate. Part of the reason waiting is so hard is because you spend most of your time in your head and not acting with your feet. So, decide to do something to move in that direction today.

Every day this week, before you put your head on your pillow, write something down in your planner or in your journal that you appreciated about the day. Where did you see God show up? Where did you experience the gift of His presence? Where did you experience beauty? Any lessons learned?

LESSON 16

Don't Believe Everything You Think

Thoughts come and go. You cannot control them. You can learn to filter them, however. You don't have to let them stay and take up residence in your mind. This is critical to our emotional wellbeing. Because not every thought that pops into your head is true. And as we think about dreams and the Divine sparks that God places in your head and heart, it is critical to know that the enemy will also make you question their validity and your capacity to accomplish them.

Laurie Beth Jones, in her book, *Jesus, Life Coach: Learn from the Best,* writes, "Once I had a dream where I was wading in a river full of snakes floating by me. I made it to the other side by not panicking and certainly by not picking up any of the snakes. Negative thoughts are like snakes. If you let them float past you, you'll be okay. But if you grab them and try to wrestle with them, you're in for some fang time."[14]

The father of lies is quite skillful at planting thoughts that are not true. He is also crafty at planting thoughts that are negative, true

14 Laurie Beth Jones, *Jesus, Life Coach: Learn from the Best,* (Nashville: Thomas Nelson, 2004), 251.

or not. You cannot control these thoughts from arising. You can control whether or not those planted lies and negative thoughts will germinate and take root, however. Lies and negative thoughts can enter our consciousness at any point. They can arise naturally. Choosing to let them stay increases the probability that they will take up residence as belief.

Don't believe everything you think.

All your thoughts are not helpful. They are not all true. Neither are all positive thoughts true. Truth is helpful. Lies are not. Of course, the $64,000 question is HOW TO DISTINGUISH between negative thoughts that aren't true and the painful thoughts that are. Doubts kill dreams. They clutter your thinking, distract your attention, and make your pursuit a burden, not a joy.

That said, there are tough-to-swallow truths that we cannot wish away. These are not negative thoughts that kill dreams. Rather, they are reality-checks that help us narrow the field of play so that we may focus on what we were really meant to pursue.

If you are to banish doubts and nurture positivity, it is crucial to understand and execute the following three key principles.. The way to defend yourself against lies infecting your belief system is what I refer to as 3D Thoughtfulness. It is a dream's best friend.

3D Thoughtfulness

De-clutter

There are many ways to do this. Like cleaning a closet, open your mind, rummage through it. Discard what you no longer find useful. Preserve what helps. Add what brings value. Make this a regular rhythm.

Daily journaling. Guided meditation. I use HeadSpace. (See lesson 3.) These two methods help you train the mind to let lies and unhelpful thoughts pass by and helpful and true thoughts stick.

Devote

God is the Father of Truth. Jesus said in a prayer to His Father, "Make them holy by your truth; teach them your word, which is truth" (New Living Translation, John 17:17).

This is most certainly true. Don't treat the Word of God as unimportant in your daily life. Don't dismiss. Don't exercise thoughtfulness without truth! You don't stand a chance without the Word of God. If you are in such a place that your can't make yourself do it, find someone who can turn you in the right direction. Have a friend who you know devotes him or herself to the Word of Truth drop you a daily text or email from their devoting time. Consider signing up for a daily text from the **YouVersion App.**[15] Remember D.E.A.R... Drop Everything And Read (the Bible) at a certain time

15 *YouVersion App,* https://www.youversion.com/the-bible-app/

in the middle of your day. Do something now to interrupt your normal thought pattern. Give it a try this week. See what happens.

Delight

"And now, dear brothers and sisters, one final thing. Fix your thoughts on what is true, and honorable, and right, and pure, and lovely, and admirable. Think about things that are excellent and worthy of praise" (New Living Translation, Philippians 4:8)

Remember the prior Lesson's Try This Section. Reserve space in the morning and in the evening to think about something excellent from your day. Consider some event, some gift, something that caught your attention and then passed. Linger there as a discipline each day until your heart is moved to praise. Praising God leaves little room for dwelling on lies and unhelpful thoughts.

If you still harbor any doubt that this works, can I simply ask you to humor me and give 3D Thoughtfulness a try this week?

TRY THIS

Give 3D Thoughtfulness a try.

De-clutter … Devote … Delight

LESSON 17

Raise a Voice of Hope

I am free to think a million different thoughts. I am no longer a slave to fear, but a child of God. I am not trapped in discouragement, but free to trust. And since God has given me this freedom, I have the power to choose hope. No matter what. As a result, I can lead others to hope.

Dreaming is tricky business. By its very nature, as something yet unseen, a dream requires hope. Hope is God's business. As such, it can easily slip through our grasp. The hope that God intends for me, a finite being, can feel like too much to bear.

I can tap into the infinite by affirming my connection with the One who sparks dreams. I can say, "Today I release my tendency to be distraught, fatigued, and inhibited." I can repeat, "Today I choose hope." And I can believe it.

Dreaming a dream and realizing it is an involved process. These simple affirmations are not a one-time magic bullet. Raising a voice of hope is not simply a matter of the will. Affirmations are only the first step in the process of raising a voice of hope. Dreams need hope to thrive. Hope beyond ourselves.

I can begin to set my mind for the journey by repeating what I know to be true. God sparks dreams. And He does so in me.

If I can learn to think differently, if I can learn to choose hope, I will be capable of raising a voice of hope. God provides me with hope-releasing moments. In the midst of my limitations and circumstances, He calls me to remember my identity, and affirm His design. Repeating the truth about who I am, and who God is, over time, I learn to think differently. And, as I learn to think differently, I can become a dreamer who raises a voice of hope.

In the middle of so much judgment and negativity, of name-calling and character assassinations, of distance and brokenness, it is easy to give into despair and join the hopeless voices that surround us. It's second nature to lose hope.

God has a dream for His people. And He has birthed that dream in our hearts. It has been this way ever since He declared Israel to be a light to the Gentiles. In order to raise the voice of hope in their time Israel would need constant reminders of their identity and His design. Call these reminders "Dream Sparks."

Consider one of these moments from one of Israel's greatest leaders, Joshua. Surrounded by godless, Gentile nations, Israel had taken possession of the Promised Land. The ways of God were distinct from those of these nations that enveloped them. Joshua stood before his people and challenged Israel to choose. Kind of like trying to stem the tide of the ways of the world, Israel was supposed to be different. Joshua said, "As for me and my house, we will serve (choose) the Lord. " (Joshua 24:15) We like to quote this passage. These words are in many homes, on plaques, given in cards. It's a bold statement. We love the sound of it. It sounds hopeful. So, we quote it.

But this oath is more than simply inspiring words. It is a critical moment of action. It is a Dream Spark moment for Israel. At Shechem Joshua calls the children of Israel to make a choice. It might seem like an easy choice to make looking back. Realizing the context of this story, though, will help you discover the common complexities that emerge for anyone who stands alone against the tide. Israel alone is supposed to represent God and His faithfulness to the godless nations that surround them.

This is another critical moment in the history of the Israelites as witnesses. It is a covenant moment. In a sense, as he leaves his people, Joshua is reminding them not turn their backs on their joyful obligation to follow the Lord and show Him to their neighbors. For this purpose they have been redeemed.

God doesn't leave them alone, however. He uses Joshua and this recommitment ceremony to help Israel remember God's benevolent generosity in spite of its inability to carry out its part of the divine agreement, which was to drive out the enemy nations from the land of promise. I guess the choice to obey God completely wasn't so simple after all. God raises a voice of hope for Israel even when they can't. And He does it with a rhythm we can replicate.

We can repeat these same steps in those inevitable dream-challenging and hope-fleeting moments that we will face. By incorporating the steps in Joshua 24 into the pursuit of our dreams, we choose to raise a voice of hope when the odds are stacked against us. God is in these steps.

Stop *(vs. 1)*

Joshua summons Israel. They stopped and presented themselves to the Lord.

Personal Application: Silence. Take a break. Conduct a divine interruption of the ordinary patterns of your living. Settle in for a sacred moment of renewal.

Ask: What do you need to stop doing or saying in order to be truly present for this moment?

Recall *(vs. 2-13)*

Joshua quotes God as He retells His redemptive story.

Personal Application: Remember and recount your personal experience with God's faithfulness. Write down real-place, real-time moments. Remembering is critical because without it we cannot feel and express proper gratitude. Furthermore, out of memory hope grows.

Ask: Which of God's promises do you need to remember to keep hope flourishing?

Declare *(vs. 14-15)*

Joshua challenges Israel to declare its allegiance to God. Spoken out loud this covenant moment propels Israel forward. Joshua goes first. And commands Israel to choose.

Personal Application: Consider who or what will get your allegiance and choose.

Ask: What affirmation do you need to speak aloud or make public?

Discard *(vs. 22-23)*

Joshua commands Israel to throw away all other allegiances by destroying their idols.

Personal Application: Put away the comfortable, but complacent patterns that you have given yourself over to. These can be thoughts, patterns, distractions, anything that has kept you from dreaming.

Ask: How will you remove these hope-stealing thoughts and reminders that are keeping you down?

Make It Visible *(vs. 25-27)*

Joshua recorded the events of this covenant renewal in the Book of God's Instruction. And, he places a rock there. He leaves them with a visible record and sign so they will never forget.

Personal Application: Write down your renewed intention. Inscribe it on your heart by making it visible.

Ask: What tangible reminder of this moment can you place in your line of site that will take you back to this renewal moment?

A leader who repeatedly goes back to God's promises and faithfulness to deliver on those promises "chooses hope this day" and becomes a confident, hope-filled leader even in the most uncertain times.

Joshua had reason to hope. Unlike his neighbors, he and his household had chosen to align themselves with the Lord and His purpose because He had always been faithful. He had chosen allegiance to God because God had chosen him.

There is a parallel here that I want to make sure we don't miss.

Joshua says to the Israelites, Don't turn your back on your obligation to the Lord to be His witnesses. After all, didn't God explicitly say, You ARE My witnesses. I have given you the capacity to show Me to the world?

In like manner, I am saying to you, Don't turn your back on your capacity to dream. God has placed His dream in your heart.

You not only have the capacity to dream, you have a joyful obligation to dream.

Discovering a dream and seeing it through to realization is part of your covenant with God. God wants us to be dreamers, to tap into the freedom that He gives, to experience the fullness of Him, to conceive of and give birth to a dream as a testament to Him.

There will be many times in your leadership that you will be given a choice to raise a voice of hope or continue to grind under the weight of fear. You have reason to hope too. God is your leader.

Allow me to get personal for a moment. Raising a voice of hope is not natural for me. Sure, I dream. But I also doubt. I am quick to chastise myself. I am reminded daily of circumstantial and personal limitations. I can give you many more reasons why *I can't* than why *I will*.

These simple steps from Joshua's life have helped me choose hope. You can find reminders of renewal moments strewn all over my home and office space. On my closet doors in my home office you can read post-it notes of affirmation. You will discover painted rocks on my desk and 3 x 5 cards taped to my mirror. You will see phrases that have become mantras of hope written on my dry erase boards. These visible stepping stones lift my hope again and again.

In those covenant moments we hear again and again of God's faithfulness in our history. And we get to choose again. At God's initiative we get to change our mind, put aside our hope-killing ways, declare our allegiance, and raise a voice of hope.

TRY THIS

Pay close attention to your thoughts today. Hopeful or Fearful? What might you do today to raise a voice of hope, even if only an inner voice? Perhaps in these moments God is calling you to another covenant moment. **Stop. Recall. Declare. Discard. Make it visible.**

Then, be aware of the spaces you occupy throughout the day. Where can you raise a voice of hope? Where can you call others to their covenant moment?

At the end of day... reflect on the situations you found yourself in and how you handled them. In addition, account for your thoughts. What happened for you today as you lived out your day in response to your covenant moment?

I Will Not Overcome
First World Consumeristic Christianity

My distaste for consumerism in American Christianity almost drove me to quit. God provided a sabbatical.

The church where I serve as Lead Pastor granted me a six-month sabbatical from the local parish November 2016-May 2017. It was a once-in-a-lifetime gift. I am forever grateful.

It is understandable that those who are created to be part of our Kingdom dreams strike out to pursue the American dream as well. Yet this is problematic. They don't always play well together, these two dreams, though they live side by side.

At some point during the sabbatical I gave up the fight. God released me from the pressure. Better said, He finally helped me see that it is not my responsibility to turn people from American consumerism to Kingdom pursuits. Rather, it was my privilege to love them as they lived in real tension between the two. All my efforts in my ministry to convince others of Kingdom ways didn't seem to work. As a matter of fact, all my personal efforts to resolve this tension in my own life weren't working. God graciously revealed to me my own participation in the problem. I am a living example of the challenge of American consumerism for the follower of Jesus.

I guess God got tired of me whining and complaining because he led me to greater understanding and empathy. He began to challenge me to work within the context of American consumerism. This is where I live. And these are the people with whom I live. I do not live in a different reality. Jesus has called me to pursue His dream in this context.

Missionaries work within their context, not above it.

America is my mission field. Consumerism is one of the realities of America, part of the context.

To effectively engage the people in the context of where we live, we must choose to live in love and without judgment. The scripture describes this as being *in the world*, but not *of the world*. I would call these mission realities. We do not control the conversation. We do not set the agenda. We do not call the shots. We live alongside. We build trust. We listen in order to understand.

Applying these missionary realities is transformational. Leveraging those lessons within the reality of American consumerism challenges every posture I am accustomed to.

As a missionary in this American landscape, I try to listen instead of convince, love instead of judge, and learn instead of debate.

Cursing the darkness is not very effective. Shining the light is. Of course, I need to distinguish between the light and the darkness.

God will help me with discernment. I guess the point I am trying to get across here is that attempting to convince people to shed their consumeristic tendencies is tiresome.

Celebrating the glorious and gracious nature of God is inviting.

This American mission field reality is not only a reality outside the walls of the church. It is also prevalent within those walls. Constantly pointing out the emptiness of consumerism will not rid the church of it. That approach will not convince Christians to recalculate. The desire for more, after all, is built into our DNA by God. God put a deep desire into the heart of every person for more of Him. It's the divine thumbprint marking mortal creatures as His.

The problem with consumerism is that it is a replacement for God and any replacement will ultimately disappoint. You cannot serve both God and mammon. But constantly pointing this out to a group of people who are largely satisfied with what consumerism has delivered is an uphill battle. If our dream as Christian leaders is to live out an inclusive Kingdom Dream, one that embraces God's children who are steeped in this culture, then perhaps adjusting our approach to better communicate the dream is a worthy pursuit. Here are a few ideas to challenge our preconceptions.

Compare and Contrast Without Judgment

Just the facts, ma'am!

Instead of lashing out against the consumeristic reality, leverage it.

Bright and shiny propped up with creative and powerful marketing versus real and authentic. Sustainable and true weathers the storm, nurtures the soul, warms stone-cold hearts. In other words, uncover the end result of consumerism. It is a common experience for all of us. All of the substitutes for God wear out. They need to be replaced. God-substitutes fray and disintegrate. God endures!

And if our greatest testimony to the world is our transformed lives as followers of Jesus, then we must share our real-life redemption stories and our accounts of how our lives have been changed. There is a challenge with this. If we as a church do not reflect Divine Light in our personal narratives, then we will be forced to use the advertising world's bright and shiny methods to get the word out. And by such methods, we would come across as inauthentic, transactional instead of transformational.

So, compare and contrast the Kingdom ways of Jesus with the ways of American consumerism. Again, just the facts, baby! Don't try so hard to convince. Show, don't tell. Let the real life stories stand. Allow them space to do their work.

Work Tirelessly to Show the Beauty of God

I will never be able to beat the bright and shiny. But I can work a little harder at shining the light on the true Original. Recently I read a Facebook post that pointed out the lack of creativity in movie productions these days. Every movie seems to be a retread of past scripts. Ecclesiastes 1:9 "...there is nothing new under the sun." Ah. I think we're on to something.

God's character is astounding. Utilize the Divine DNA given to you to creatively and winsomely direct peoples' gaze to His beauty. He is the One and Only, the Original. Your Kingdom dream centers on Him, not on anything or anyone else.

Rely on God for creativity. After all, He is the Creator. Any created thing has Him as its source. He put the ability to create in us. Creativity is a divine DNA marker. Use that to give HIM glory. Don't settle for the created thing. (Romans 1:23, 25)

Become a Master Story Connector

God is THE master storyteller. Don't tell His story without connecting it to ours. And don't tell our stories without connecting them to His. Our stories are forever intertwined.

God's redemptive story shows in blinding reality the ultimate destiny of choosing God's dream over man's. Time and again throughout human history, God shows us what the results of consumerism are. Our human dreams die. They come to an end. He also shows us the results of His enduring love. His dream never dies. It overcomes our fallenness. Connect these biblical stories to ours. Connect the past with the present as you lead people into the future. Use stories, both old and new, as evidence for the need to dream God's dream. And don't tell any story without making the connection to that dream.

TRY THIS

Spend an evening taking notes on the commercials you watch on TV. What are the products promising? Over the course of the evening how many different competing messages do you pick up that stand against the Kingdom ways of Jesus?

Spend some time in prayer asking God to fill you with love for the people who sometimes get caught up in these worldly promises. Ask Him to help you observe without judgment and to love without restraint.

LESSON 19

The Limitations of Scarcity Mentality

Jesus said to His "children"... the disciples, "You will do greater things than me" (New Living Translation, John 14:12).

Your children will surpass you. I'm referring to both your biological children and anyone you invest in and feel a sense of responsibility for.

If you're doing it right, there is an exponential aspect to your investment.

"Consider how helping others achieve success (however you/they decide to define it) results in significant benefits in a number of directions:

- The receiver reaches a far greater potential than they would have on his/her own.
- The world is bettered and is given a life-giving model to emulate.
- The giver is remembered fondly and is often publicly (and privately) thanked for their contribution.

- The original recipient is more likely to "pay it forward," endowing others as he/she has been endowed.
- And the cycle begins again."[16]

This is why it is more critical to help others grow than it is to achieve success ourselves.

The main culprit that keeps us from helping others? Scarcity Mentality, the belief that what we have is not enough, and that if we don't preserve and protect it, it will be gone forever. Worst-case scenario dominates our thinking. This mindset leads us to possessiveness and fear, the foundations of greed. We become the opposite of what we aspire to be: more generous.

Unfortunately, this is a completely natural phenomenon. It happens to all of us in one way or another. We're not alone and we're not helpless either. We receive help from on high. The King of our dreams wants us to experience more. He wants us to experience the fullness of His life so the world can know His life. And He gives us that fullness. Though He is not limited by a scarcity mentality, He chooses to work within our natural constraints. Isn't that amazing?

The gifts of God multiply, and they don't expire. They don't run out. God is NEVER short on supply. Isn't this one of the main points of the miracle of the loaves and the fish in Mark 6: 30-34. "You feed them," Jesus said. Give them what you have.

There was a time in my preaching ministry when I was using books by expert Christian authors to shape our sermon series. I was afraid

---

16 Joshua Becker, *Why Helping Others Succeed Can Be Your Greatest Success,* https://www.becomingminimalist.com/helping-others-succeed/.

that what God was leading me to say was not profound enough. One of the members of my congregation came to me and lovingly challenged me to trust in what God was giving me to share. "You are our pastor. God has given you what He wants to share with us. I don't need to hear what someone else says."

Once the wounded pride dissipated, I was able to consider what she said. Today, I am not as quick to go hunting for the expert's quote as I was before that encouraging confrontation. I am much more willing to trust the thought or insight that God has given to me. Recently, in our preacher's learning community at our Church we were challenging each other to "commit to the bit." It's a term used by actors and comedians when they get a crazy idea. Go for it. Trust your instincts. Go all in and don't hesitate. I am thankful for that moment when I was challenged to find and share *my* voice. After all, God gave it to me for a reason, right?

Now don't get me wrong. It is good to share insights, even a whole series of thoughts, from published authors. That said, I encourage you to find your own voice. With Jesus, what you have been given is ALWAYS enough.

When we talk about dreams it is natural for us to think about our own dream as a personal opportunity to shine, even outshine others. Yet, in this lesson, I really want us to tap into the desire to do the opposite: to be outshined! I think most parents understand this. Can you imagine how much it would empower our communities if we could extend the kind of trust and confidence in God's provision to others that parents extend to their children?

Our aim, then, our goal is to invest in others so they surpass us. This gives honor to God's way. This gives testimony to the Kingdom of Jesus!

TRY THIS

Who...are you sensing an opportunity to invest in?

What...do you have to offer that will help them surpass you?

LESSON 20

Embracing Limitations
Drives Creativity

Standing in Walgreens trying to pick a deodorant, I get overwhelmed. I mean, really, how could there be so many deodorants? All the choices make me freeze with indecision. Cereal. Pasta. Wine. Bottled Water...

More options are not always better.

Hearing that God has called upon us to reach out to the world can have the same inhibitive effect. When we understand that our vocation is to spread His Word, we often become paralyzed with the same indecision. *Where to begin? How to be most effective?* All the possibilities engender thoughts, but also second thoughts, and those second thoughts bog us down. That's why at the Church we use phrases like "embrace limitations" and "accept responsibility" for your "walkable community."[17]

In art school while pursuing his dream, Phil Hansen developed an uncontrollable shake in his hand. The shake came about after years of drawing using tiny little dots (called pointillism). He describes this

---

17 Paul Sparks, Tim Soerens, and Dwight J. Friesen, *The New Parish, How Neighborhood Churches are Transforming Mission, Discipleship, and Community*, (Madison: IVP, 2014).

time in his life as doomsday. His dream was crushed. For a while he tried to control the shake by gripping his pencil tighter and tighter. The pain in his hand and joints increased and eventually he quit art school and quit art.

Months later, unable to let art go, Hansen went to see a neurologist who told him two things. "You have permanent nerve damage." And, "Why don't you embrace the shake?"

So he did.

Drawing on some of the same concepts in pointillism – for instance, using fragments to create a unified picture – he began just letting his hand go. He stopped trying to control the shake. He felt free. He discovered that the squiggly lines that he now produced could become components of beautiful portraits. They weren't the dots he had grown accustomed to using, but they could still create new masterpieces. From there he began experimenting with larger mediums and even used his feet to create images.

"After having gone to a single approach to art, I ended up having an approach to creativity that completely changed my artistic horizon." he said in his Ted Talk.[18] He ultimately discovered that there was an endless future of possibilities for his art.

Constraints often help us tighten our focus. And, when focus tightens, horizons expand.

---

18 Phil Hansen, *Embrace the Shake,* (TED Talk, May 21, 2013), https://youtu.be/YrZTho_o_is.

The Apostle Paul never tells us what infirmity he was dealing with. Yet he wanted the Lord to take it away. In a sense, the Lord, tells Paul the same thing the neurologist told Phil Hansen.

Three different times I begged the Lord to take it away. Each time he said, "My grace is all you need. My power works best in weakness." So now I am glad to boast about my weaknesses, so that the power of Christ can work through me. That's why I take pleasure in my weaknesses, and in the insults, hardships, persecutions, and troubles that I suffer for Christ. For when I am weak, then I am strong. (New Living Translation, 2 Corinthians 12:8-10)

"Embracing the limitation can actually drive creativity," says Hansen.[19]

It is only in embracing limitations and letting go of desired outcomes that you can tap into creativity at deep levels.

How many times have you not produced content because you were afraid it wouldn't be good enough? How many times have you not realized the thought because you already determined it wasn't going to be well-received by others? We define ourselves by how we think the "portrait" is going to turn out. It is a painful, self-defeating way to live.

What we have is not enough, we think. I see this all the time. It's subtle. In some of our supportive discipleship environments where we attempt to stimulate creativity and experimentation in living our lives with Gospel intentionality I hear phrases like these all the time.

19 *ibid.*

"I don't know if this counts or not, but I was thinking..."

"Not sure if this would ever work or not, so I've been hesitant to try it."

"I've been thinking for a while that I should... But, I just don't think it is enough."

"But if I do start, I'm not sure I will be able to back it up. I don't know enough."

Help me think this through. The boy's lunch in the feeding of the five thousand. Moses stumbling and struggling with his speech impediment in Pharaoh's Egypt. Mud and spit in the hands of the Savior. Tax collectors, fishermen, prostitutes, Peter who couldn't stand up to the pressure from a little girl, David the shepherd boy and later the liar, cheater, abuser of power, adulterer, and murderer.

Every single one of these stories had a divine purpose and a limited or flawed conduit. God chose to work through materials at hand.

With God's help, we will find a way with the resources at our disposal. We shouldn't expect that some sort of magical windfall is the only means of achieving our goals. We probably possess the means from the get-go. The real challenge is to accept that which is already within us, to accept that we, even at our most limited, are still vessels for His will.

God is always calling those who are limited. He embraces limitations. He uses the ordinary.

Teddy Roosevelt is credited with saying, "Do what you can with what you have where you are."

Why does embracing your shake drive creativity?

Embracing your shake...

...allows the Creator to shine.

By not relying on a bunch of man-made materials, (don't take a purse or anything with you, Mark 6:8, etc., etc.) you put the art in the hand of the Creator! And, He allows you to create WITH HIM!

God is an "ex nihilo" God.

Creating something from our limitations is perhaps the closest we can ever get to creating like God creates.

If God can make the entire universe out of nothing (the void), imagine what he can do with your "something," even though you may regard it as severely limited, paltry, or insufficient.

...allows you to start with what you have instead of delaying in hope of something better.

WE all have limitations, weaknesses. If we determine that those weaknesses will keep us from creating, we will not create anything. Only in embracing those limitations can we get started.

...permits the real you to emerge.

As unique as your limitations are, so too is your unique output. No add-ons. No substitutes, compensations, or enhancements. Just you and what you got.

So, what is **your** limitation? Right now, what is keeping you from dreaming big and realizing?

Lack of know-how?

Not enough money?

No experience?

Not enough time?

What would happen if you simply acknowledged the reality of your limitation, but instead of letting it block you, you allowed it to have some bearing on your way forward? Perhaps it would necessitate a slight detour. Or perhaps it would inspire you to summon stronger resolve and plow straight ahead.

This book had its genesis by confining my writing to 5-6am every morning. The time limitations sparked creativity.

TRY THIS

Pick a limitation. Lean into it.

Offer it to God by using it.

Watch Phil Hansen's TED Talk and consider which personal limitation you can overcome by embracing it.

What's one way you could move forward *with* this limitation today?

Give it a shot.

The Big Two: Unwavering Belief and Vigorous Execution

Nothing is accomplished in life without two essentials, conviction and execution.

On the one hand, if you lack mental certitude that what you are doing is yours to do, you will lack the resolve to weather the inevitable storms. Stake a claim and accept the responsibility for your dream.

On the other hand, if you lack the plan to succeed, you will be distracted from that thing you are to be doing. You must commit to the strategies, plans, and meaningful action.

Unwavering belief and vigorous execution of a plan are both essential to achieve anything worthwhile. The former has to do with mindset. The latter, lifestyle. Without unwavering belief you will become discouraged. Without the vigorous execution you will become distracted.

Discouragement and distraction are production killers.

I have found that the proper mindset and appropriate life-giving habits must be integrated into my daily life rhythms if I want to succeed. If I ever hope to stay the course I must know in my heart that the goal in front of me is worth pursuing. And I will need to execute the right plan, which may entail fostering the right habits and compiling the right action items day by day, to attain my goal.

Mindset and lifestyle are huge. Just because your dream gets God's approval and is clearly worth the effort, that doesn't mean that it will go unchallenged. Not once, or every once in awhile, but relentlessly. Consistently, persistently challenged. Obstacles, distractions, detours are all a part of our daily pursuit of worthwhile goals. The dream will draw challenges on both of these critical aspects, mindset and lifestyle.

Write down your goal in this sentence:

"I will _____ , no matter what. There is no other option."[20]

This is the place to start. Fervent belief in your cause is the foundational gift that you will build upon. So, put this cause, this dream to the test. How will the world be different if you do not pursue this dream? If not this dream, then what? If not you then who? What will be missing from the world if you do not pursue this dream? How did you come about this dream? How was it given to you? Why you? What will happen to you if you do not pursue it? A dream without a plan is powerless. A plan without the will to be realized is empty.

---

20 Hal Elrod and Steve Scott, *The Miracle Morning for Writers: How to Build a Writing Ritual that Increases Your Impact and Your Income.* (Miracle Morning, 2016), 177.

Two things keep leaders unsettled.

Dreaming without a plan.

Planning without a dream.

Dreams are crucial. BUT we only glance at them. We only look up occasionally to see that we are on track.

Plans are vital. We abide by them. We order our days by them. Schedule them. Focus and finish them. If they aren't proving to be effective, we adjust them or change them.

"Our goals can only be reached through a vehicle of a plan, in which we must fervently believe, and upon which we must vigorously act. There is no other route to success"[21]

Dreams need to work hand-in-hand with plans if they are to be measurable so that you can determine if you are making progress. But only if they hold their proper place. The dream is not the plan. The plan is not the dream. Both have their place. The dream is a future reality that remains out there somewhere in the distance that inspires our pursuit. The plan is the step-by-step process in the present tense that keeps us on track and gives us the chance to realize the dream.

If we don't keep these straight and distinct, we will fall victim to confusion. Thinking the plan is the dream results in rigidity, busyness, drudgery. Thinking the dream is the plan results in victimization (self-pity), daydreaming, wishful thinking.

---

21 Pablo Picasso, (Best Self Journal, 2015-2016), 27. https://bestself.co/

If I don't undergird the dream with the support structure of quantifiable steps, the dream will fade, even become loathsome. Break the dream down. What will it take in the first year to begin the journey toward the dream? I'm here. I want to go there. What are my first steps? The journey to Breckenridge, CO from Madison, WI begins in Madison and takes me down Hwy 151/18, first past Mt. Horeb, Barneveld, Dodgeville, Platteville and then through the rolling hills leading to Dubuque, IA. Figure out your route. What are the things that must happen in Year One if you hope to arrive at your destination in Year Five? Establish that Year One objective.

Then, break down that Year One objective into smaller steps. I find it helpful to look at 90 day or quarterly objectives. Begin with the first 90 days, or quarter. Visualize this as getting to Dubuque on your way to Breckenridge. This provides direction toward the dream while not overwhelming you with the entirety of the trip. Living and planning one year out is too long a time frame. The rate and pace of change is too fast.

Follow these steps:

1. Articulate a major Year One objective.

What is the one thing I must accomplish in Year One to have a chance at attaining my ultimate dream?

2. Determine your next 90-day/12-week/quarterly objectives.

What is the one thing I must accomplish in this 90-day season to have a chance at hitting my one year objective?

3. Figure out what measurable tactics, habits, goals, action initiatives you will need to implement to achieve the 90-day objective.

What are the daily and weekly action steps/ habits I need to build into my calendar?

4. Work those smaller initiatives into your daily schedule.

TRY THIS

How would you fill in the blank?

I will _____ no matter what. There is no other option.

Answer these questions in your journal:

What is keeping you from believing fervently?

Where do you need help in order to grow in executing a plan?

Now start planning your dream.

One-Year Objective:

90-day Objective:

Tactics/Habits/Goals/Action Initiatives:

LESSON 22

Unsettled Leaders
Need Dream Catchers

I am not a proponent of the theology behind the dream catcher. With a little tweak, however, it serves as a powerful metaphor for one of the most basic and underperformed leadership skills. (If you have trouble thinking about this because of the theology, then think about a spider web instead.)

The twofold idea is that we catch what sparks and filter out what snuffs. Many unsettled leaders have lost the ability to dream. Or they never developed the ability to dream in the first place. Or they have a dream, but are unable to realize it because they have become inhibited by fear.

Dreaming is an essential part of effective leadership. The inability to dream is the root cause of feeling unsettled. God inspires dreams. He is always doing something new. He invites us to co-create with Him. Dreaming inspires hope. It gives us a direction and activates faith. It inspires trust in God's provision. It puts us in the position of total dependence on God. Call it dreaming. Call it vision. Whatever you call it, unsettled leaders struggle to do it. Why?

They're told not to.

They think they don't have time for it. Or they think it's selfish.

I just received an email from a coaching client. He has been on this journey with me for some time now. In that process he has rekindled a desire to take steps toward achieving a personal dream. In his heartfelt email he closed with this line: "I'm mainly thinking out loud trying to justify personal goals in midst of seemingly consuming work goals and schedule."

We should never feel the need to justify personal goals and dreams! It is not selfish to follow Jesus and have that following impact our personal lives! God has endowed us with the desire to dream personal dreams that impact our lives for good. He has made it part of our DNA!

Take a moment right now and open the Bible to Deuteronomy 8. Start with verse 7 and read through verse 10. Now, what would this dream have meant to the original recipients? What would this description of a future land have meant for them in their historical context? What difference would that dream have meant for their living and hoping in the present moment? The language! This is just one example of where God vividly describes a future. In life-giving detail He lays it out. He spares no creativity because He is the God of creation.

So, why would God not want you, who bear His image, to exercise your own creativity through dreaming?

But you are a responsible person, who believes responsibility trumps risk. And there are duties to fulfill, obligations to carry out. Dreams are risky business, a distraction from paying the bills. If you're not careful, you will lose what you have been so responsible in gaining.

A voice pipes up, you'll never realize the dream anyway, so, why even try? But this is the wolf in sheep's clothing, fear disguised as prudence.

Two things are necessary to break the bad habits that have emerged because of these fears. (Dream Catcher)

Let the good stuff stick. *(Catch the dream. Grab on to it.) Learning how to dream (again) free from fear.* **Let the life-stealing stuff flow on by.** *(Through the in-between space, let it pass.)*

TRY THIS

Ask yourself these questions:

1. If anything were going to get in the way of me pursuing this dream, what would it be?
2. How might I be sabotaging my own pursuit? How might I be getting in the way of my own progress?
3. Who's one person right now whom I can trust to help the good stuff stick and the unhealthy stuff filter through? What do I want to ask them?
4. What's at stake if I don't pursue this? What is to gain if I do?
5. As I look at my dream, what is the next step I should take on my journey?

Choose Your Niche.
Master That

Dictionary.com defines niche as "a place or position suitable or appropriate for a person or thing." Or "a distinct segment of the market."

By nature we are copycats. We see someone else succeed and our focus shifts. We no longer pay attention to what WE are doing. We obsess over what that successful person is doing. It's impossible to discover our own unique dream when we are focusing attention on copying someone else's.

What makes this challenge even more difficult to overcome is that we live in a society that compels us to conform. "You ought to be that kind of business owner, this kind of dad, this kind of writer, that kind of pastor." And so, if we cannot choose our own craft, focus on our unique contribution, or list the things we are placed on this earth to do with proper clarity, we remain vulnerable to the expectations of others.

God created you a masterpiece. You are one of a kind. (Ephesians 2:10) You are designed intentionally and for a great purpose. You have been set apart to contribute something no one else can.

Attempting to compete with someone else at their game is not wise. Begin the search for your dream, by embracing your niche. God placed you there for a reason.

"The challenge here is to choose your craft. Focus on the thing — or portfolio of things — that only you can do. And do it well, without apology or complaint."[22]

There will be a void in the world if you don't. There are already a million people doing what others want you to do. It is their fear that drives them to keep you stuck playing their game. Think about this for a moment. Here, I'll repeat it. It is their fear that drives them to keep you stuck playing their game. You are already well aware of how your own fear keeps you from dreaming. Don't add others' fear to the mix!

There are people around you who have never discovered their own niche. They will want you to fit their mold because it will make them feel better about themselves. There are people who are afraid to dream. They settle instead for compliance. They will want you to comply. Theirs is the business of control and credit. Resist this business. Resist them.

Author Jeff Goins goes on to write "Recently, a friend shared with me a time when he was running a marathon and watching all these people pass him. He was frustrated, because he thought he was in good shape, but here he was, struggling to keep up with the pack.

---

22 Jeff Goins, *Stop Running the Wrong Race and Choose Your Own Craft*, (Goins, Writer), https://goinswriter.com/choose-craft.

Just as my friend was on the verge of calling it quits, someone came alongside him and said, 'Run your own race.'"[23]

Finding your niche will require a reawakening. I would liken this process to what Julia Cameron describes as *your recovering artist.* Recovering artists have been blocked and are now striving to break free. "Don't expect blocked friends to applaud your recovery. That's like expecting your best friends from the bar to celebrate your sobriety."[24]

To choose your niche more than likely you will need to break free from your dependence on your friends' approval. And becoming a recovering artist/dreamer will mean that you may disturb the relational status quo that you once experienced with those around you.

"Blocked friends may find your recovery disturbing. Your getting unblocked raises the unsettling possibility that they, too, could become unblocked and move into authentic creative risks rather than bench-sitting cynicism. Be alert to subtle sabotage from friends. You cannot afford well-meaning doubts right now. Their doubt will reactivate your own."[25]

Believe that you were given a gift to share with the world, a unique and powerful life-transforming gift from your Creator for the benefit of others. Your first task is to discover what that is. And, I would suggest, discovering YOUR niche is a great place to start.

23 *ibid.*
24 Julia Cameron, *The Artist's Way,* 43.
25 *ibid.*

Finding your niche in and of itself can become a fear-producing pursuit. Just the idea that you have *a* niche can be alarming. As we consider dreams and the execution of those dreams in this book, we want to resist the strong pull for perfection. We are not talking about finding the perfect niche. That can be daunting. Instead of finding *the* niche, let's start with discovering *a* niche.

TRY THIS

What do you find yourself wanting to do more of? *I wish I had more time to…*

What comes naturally for you? What do you do intuitively? *I could do this in my sleep!*

Where have you provided value to others recently? What were you doing that really helped them? *I'm so grateful that I was able to help.*

Do you have compassion for others? Where does your compassion and another person's needs intersect? *I really wish that were different.*

Do you have an idea of how to improve something? *I would change that if I had the resources and time. And here's how I would do it.*

The Church Must Get Back to Mission

For the church to have an impact in the world today, it must get back to its mission. And, in order to get back to that mission, the church must learn to dream again.

Jesus established His church to be the vehicle of redemption and restoration, drawing people back to their Creator. It is the power of that dream for the world that ignites the daily work of the mission. Without that spark, the church settles for duty and obligation. Duty and obligation live in the realm of the law for most people. The call to mission is exhilarating. The mission of the church is THE adventure of adventures. It belongs in the realm of dreams. And I'm not talking about pipe dreams. I'm talking about clear and compelling direction. The second part of this book discusses the execution of the dream. Certainly there is a need for focused and relentless execution of any mission for it to succeed. And yet, the mission derives its energy from the dream.

Mission Is the Mission

The Church's mission has always been to make Jesus followers who make Jesus followers. This is the fruit that Jesus designed the church to produce. Always has been the mission, always will be the mission. A number of consecutive generations' worth of mission creep will not change that.

The mission is not to grow a church. It is not to plant a church. It is not to get people to come to church. These are only *input effects* of connecting others to Jesus.

Our mission is simply to help people follow Jesus. This is our privilege. Unfortunately, too often we have our heads down as we do our work and lose sight of this joyful opportunity.

In Matthew 12, Jesus is walking with His disciples on the Sabbath. Along the way, they get in trouble with the Pharisees for picking heads of grain. No one works on the Sabbath. It's the law. In His exchange with these religious leaders of the day, Jesus has His own mission-recalibration moment with them. He says simply, "There is something greater than the Temple. And you're looking at Him."

Can you imagine the energy it must have taken to maintain the Temple? The money to raise. The people to recruit. The programs and rituals to execute. The building needs to oversee.

And in the process you miss me, the Messiah.

As a modern-day Christian leader, I think I can imagine the energy it must have taken. I've lived it. I have had years of experience raising money, recruiting people, designing and implementing programs, protecting and executing rituals, and overseeing the maintenance of buildings. All of this demands attention. And sometimes for a Christian leader it can become the end instead of the means.

The single mission of leaders in the Church of Jesus is to help people follow Jesus and assist them in their helping others do the same.

And yet, many times we reveal our desperate need to get back to the mission by what we measure as success: ABC – attendance, buildings, cash. Sure, these measurements can give us some indication of the provisions we have been given to accomplish the mission, and give us some measure of effectiveness. Yet we can have remarkable results in these areas and still not be accomplishing the mission of the church.

The Mission is Sparked by a Dream

The dream of a world restored to its original design fuels the daily mission of the church. Our daily activity (mission) of helping others follow Jesus will be the only activity that drives us to the dream of a new creation, a restored people, a life-giving community. I long for this mission to be lived out with passion by every single follower of Jesus.

That's a dream that propels me forward. It is pretty ironic that this dream has not been widely accepted within the church. As such, it has not always been easy to hold fast to this dream. Many have preferred to just make sure the temple is taken care of, and that it prospers.

Yet I remain compelled and energized to see this dream realized. I relentlessly hold to the perspective that every aspect of life can be a platform for this exciting mission of helping people follow Jesus. Paul wrote it down for his young protégé, Timothy. "And what you have heard from me in the presence of many witnesses entrust to faithful men, who will be able to teach others also" (English Standard Version, 2 Timothy 2:2).

The church is given this exhilarating mission of helping others follow Jesus until the whole world is reunited with God and His family.

There's only one way to fix the pervasive misalignment of daily activity in the church today. The realignment starts with one person deciding to begin. One person deciding to help someone follow Jesus. And this will not happen by focusing on the execution side first. That leads to a sense of burden and feeling overwhelmed. First, it must be sparked in the heart. Stoked alive deep in the soul. Imagined in the mind. Pictured in the eyes. From there... onward.

TRY THIS

Here is one practical way YOU can start to help someone follow Jesus:

Start with a potential growth area IN YOUR JOURNEY with Jesus.

So often, in helping others follow Jesus we think about how *someone else* needs help. This can lead to a relationship of dependency. Instead, think of a spiritual growth area where YOU would like some accountability, and invite someone to join you.

Do you want to read the Bible more faithfully?

Do you want to learn how to pray?

Think about those in your life who could join you as you pursue **your goal** and invite them.

Without Relentless Singularity, Mission Creep Is Inevitable

Only with focus and grit does a dream burn through distraction.

According to the natural law of entropy, things unravel over time and gravitate towards their most disorganized state. Eventually, chaos reigns. Without consistent focus and realignment, our dreams unravel. They unravel when distractions pull us off course.

We are followers of Jesus, which means our Kingdom dream will always include the ultimate calling of disciples. And because we are leaders within this movement, our dreams will by nature of the Kingdom always be concerned with energizing Jesus-followers to pursue that dream. Every pursuit other than making disciples who make disciples is a distraction. Unfortunately, the challenge we face is just about as high as the stakes. Without persistent realignment, mission creep is a certainty.

Why is it so hard to stay the course? Why is mission creep an inevitable reality without relentless focus?

It is subtle and gradual.

We are not aware that it is happening. You could describe it as a snowball effect, or use the frog in the kettle metaphor to illustrate the reality. Mission creep is utterly imperceptible.

There are so many attractive ideas.

Ultimately most of these attractions are distractions. It is utterly impossible to say no to the good ideas if we have not discerned and devoted ourselves to the great idea. Jim Collins starts his best selling book, "Good to Great," with this helpful reminder: "Good is the enemy of great."[26]

Maybe "good" isn't so great, after all.

Many of us have never been shown how to follow Jesus.

It is very difficult to remain committed to something with relentless singularity if we have never experienced it. If we've never been in a discipling relationship, it is very easy to get distracted by ideas that are more concrete. One will almost always choose the tangible over the intangible.

For many in the church today the dream of making disciples who make disciples is an intangible pipe dream. So, we settle for the distractions. Think about this for a moment. Why do you suppose there are so many conferences within the church space on best

---

26 Jim Collins, *Good to Great: Why Some Companies Make the Leap and Others Don't,* (New York:Harper Business, 2001), 1.

practices, and model reproductions? Why so many books with formulas and systems and checklists?

Tangible trumps intangible every time. Show me how and I have a much better shot at staying the course in pursuit of my dream.

If we have never experienced the hands-on, side-by-side discovery of following Jesus, it will be less likely that we can show someone else. This is one of the major culprits when we give ourselves away to distractions.

The enemy of your soul is the master of mission creep.

He is real. He hates the Kingdom Dream. He hates the mission. His mission is to keep you pursuing ANYTHING BUT Jesus! Distraction is his #1 tactic! And, here's the kicker. He is often more focused on our "unfocusing" than we are focused on our dream.

So how can you avoid mission creep in pursuit of your Kingdom dream? As you chase after that dream, how do you remain committed to the goal of Jesus's clear mission?

Learn to recognize mission creep.

It's not *if*, it's *when*. You cannot avoid mission creep. It is inevitable. What you can do, however, is identify patterns in your own life and leadership that indicate mission creep so that you can react vigilantly and nip it in the bud. Once you can identify the patterns then you can recognize it when it is happening. This simple yet difficult first step will give you the best shot at making the necessary adjustments to stay the course.

Here are three common patterns in my leadership:

1. Getting caught up in the wrong goals and pursuits and measuring myself by the wrong metric, which makes hard work inefficient at best, counterproductive at worst.
2. Dismissing stories of discipling relationships as anecdotal.
3. Permitting the bulk of leadership conversations to be about the ABC's.(Attendance, Buildings, Cash) instead of nurturing a disciple-making culture.

Zero In on the Bullseye

Be certain what you are aiming for. Clarify it. Name it. Measure it.

Develop environments and systems that produce it. For example, how could you reshape your "devotional" time at the beginning of Board Meetings to help people follow Jesus? Have them read the Scripture for themselves and share one or two takeaways from the passage with the rest of the group. You're already good at creating environments. You've figured out how to fill the seats, balance the budget, get more people to sign up, publicize the program. Now it is time to help Jesus followers follow Jesus, and help their friends do the same.

TRY THIS;

Find your own dream. Find your own rhythm.

How do/will you follow Jesus?

Who do/will you help others follow Jesus?

Spell Out Your HOW and Your WHO

Our dreams will contribute to the Great Commission, to the command to go and make disciples. This charge has been given to every Jesus follower. Our general calling is to *glorify God and make disciples*. *To glorify God and make disciples* is a phrase I use in my consulting work with my Auxano[27] teammates when we work with churches and organizations. We start here because it is a given. We put the assumed general purpose on the table so that we can affirm it and then begin the fun work of drilling down to help this body of believers discern his or her unique part in contributing to the whole.

It is no different for you. Your unique calling will be the foundation from which your dreams will emerge. And your dream will contribute to the general call to glorify God and make disciples. This is a great filter through which to analyze whether or not your dream originates in God. Ask yourself, "Will this dream glorify God and make disciples?" How so?

It is *my* dream that this book will play a role, however modest, in sparking a movement of dreamers. I long to see followers of Jesus

---

27 Auxano, https://www.auxano.com/

dream again, this time without fear, without hesitation. Can you imagine it? Do you see it? The result would be overwhelming. What would happen if every follower of Jesus had a clearer understanding of how his or her dream contributed to the greater whole of glorifying God and making disciples? That reality would fire a movement that could not be stopped.

Spell it out. Are you beginning to see your *How* and your *Who*?

- **How** is your dream glorifying God and making disciples?
- **Who** is going to benefit from your dream becoming a reality?

There are times in our lives when we will not be serving in our sweet spot. We will be called on to give and contribute in spaces and places that take us out of our comfort zone. And, as a result, we will grow as we are stretched. We may even find our sweet spot in those challenging calls. It may be the way God helps us discover what we were meant to do.

Ultimately, our dream will align with our giftedness. Our unique calling will utilize our strength and competence. So, don't be afraid to explore and discover who you are uniquely designed to be and then pursue your dream with great freedom and vigor. That's what the Part 2 of the book is all about: the realization.

If you are struggling to sift through all of the layers upon layers of expectations of others concerning your calling, your giftedness, perhaps this is the time to invest in yourself to discover who you are and why you are. If you are interested in this, may I suggest an in-depth, personal discovery journey called Life Younique?[28]

TRY THIS

The more specific your answers to these questions the more helpful it will be to you.

How is your dream glorifying God and making disciples?

<u>How</u> are you specifically contributing to the greater Kingdom cause?

I contribute by _____.

Here's a list of possibilities to get you started: *nurturing, aligning, uplifting, saving, uniting, training, strengthening, sharpening, encouraging, writing, singing, speaking, networking, counseling, coaching, leading...*

Describe in detail how any of these may appropriately describe your contribution.

Who is going to benefit from your dream becoming a reality?

<u>Who</u> are YOUR peeps?

Here's a list of possibilities to get you started:

28 Younique, http://www.lifeyounique.com/

Teachers, entrepreneurs, families, couples, communities, trainers, the discouraged, the creatives, leaders, children, pastors, dechurched, designers, coaches, students

Once you have named your WHO, take some time and brainstorm a list of what they value .

What is most important to them?

Here's a list of possibilities to get you started:

Freedom, security, significance, creativity, empowering others, helping others, education, honesty, financial independence, impact, discernment

Finally, narrow your brainstormed list down to the top four values.

Now you will be able to fill out the following:

I contribute to Jesus' Kingdom mission by (place your *How* here)__

_____.

The people who benefit the most from my dream are (place your *Who* here) _____.

And, those people value

1.

2.

3.

4.

LESSON 27

Paper Is a Tree
Wanting to Be a Tree Again

A friend of mine works in the paper industry. One afternoon as we were swapping stories he dropped a little factoid about how paper is made that has stuck with me and, unexpectedly perhaps, given me a handle on hope in difficult times.

I always knew that paper was made from trees. Those trees are harvested, broken down into little microscopic particles. Then those particles are roughed up and for a specific reason. See, it is in their nature to want to come back together again. It is the roughing up that makes the connection so strong when they do reunite. Without being roughed up, those fibers cannot reconnect. No roughed up and reconnected tree particles, no paper.

God created us in His image. We have been roughed up because of our sin. Yet, it is in our DNA to be connected to our Creator.

We were designed by God to be in harmonious relationship with one another. Our relationships have been roughed up because of sin. It is in our DNA to be re-connected to one another.

We were designed by God to be at peace with ourselves. Our self-worth and understanding have been roughed up because of sin. It is in our DNA, however, to be whole.

When we are reunited by the grace and mercy of God in Jesus, it is a bond that sticks. And it is a reunion with God, with others, and with self. All of these relationships are vital for dreamers. Our dreams touch all three.

Once reconnected, we are then a useful page upon which God can write. He can inscribe His name, His thoughts, His Word on us for all the world to read. Paul wrote this reminder to the Jesus-followers in Corinth, "Clearly, you are a letter from Christ showing the result of our ministry among you. This 'letter' is written not with pen and ink, but with the Spirit of the living God. It is carved not on tablets of stone, but on human hearts" (New Living Translation, 2 Corinthians 3:3).

God cannot write His dream on our hearts unless we have been roughed up and reunited.

Our dreams plumb depth of meaning and find strength in this paper-making word picture.

God has implanted His Dream DNA in each of us. You were designed to dream.

So many of us don't dare to dream because all we see is brokenness and limitations. Yet, it is IN that brokenness that He prepares us, just like paper, to be a beautiful letter for the world to read.

Dreams are found as frequently within brokenness as they are within reparation and reconciliation.

Break me, melt me, mold me, fill me, use me, inscribe upon me.

Dreams are written on our lives for others' benefit as well as for ours.

All praise to God, the Father of our Lord Jesus Christ. God is our merciful Father and the source of all comfort. He comforts us in all our troubles so that we can comfort others. When they are troubled, we will be able to give them the same comfort God has given us. For the more we suffer for Christ, the more God will shower us with his comfort through Christ. Even when we are weighed down with troubles, it is for your comfort and salvation! For when we ourselves are comforted, we will certainly comfort you. Then you can patiently endure the same things we suffer. We are confident that as you share in our sufferings, you will also share in the comfort God gives us (New Living Translation, 2 Corinthians 1:3-7).

God's comfort is restorative and dream-producing. It is an unstoppable force that moves from one person to another. What an amazingly powerful thing to behold. And you are right in the middle of it.

So, the lesson here is not only to embrace your challenges, but also to search for God's dream spark there. Lean into your rough places. Examine your relationship with God. Take a long, hard look at the patterns of brokenness in human relationships. Get well acquainted with your own internal battles. Within these difficulties, you may just find a dreamer waiting to be recognized.

TRY THIS

Go to those rough places.

- Relationship with God
- Relationship with Others
- Relationship with Self

Think about a time when you were roughed up.

Think about patterns that reveal brokenness.

How do these areas impact your dream? How might they be used by God to share His redemptive nature with others? What would happen if you *leaned into* these instead of leaning *away* from them? What would happen if you surrendered them to God and let Him inscribe his message on your heart?

Any dreams sparking?

Write them down.

Consider what a reconnected, re-solidified bond might mean, one stronger than before and more useful for God's inscription.

Writing Is Important

To dream, you need to know what you want. To know what you want, you need to know who you are. Like the strong foundation of a beautiful building, writing helps you discover your truth and essence. Dreams are built upon it.

The Writing Promise

Writing is good for the soul.

Writing reveals hidden treasure.

Writing clarifies complexities.

Writing unearths the dream and gives it shape.

Can you imagine the truths of the world, of the human condition, of God's promises WITHOUT the written Word?

Threefold Gifts of Writing

Cleansing

Most diet plans or healthy eating regiments begin with a cleanse period. This is designed to get the toxins out and to establish a healthy foundation upon which to build a new routine. Think of writing in this way. The writing discipline allows us to get out what has been lurking in the recesses of our minds. It brings up and gets out thoughts that have been dormant. It shines a light on what has been in the shadows. You can't grasp what is indiscernible. You cannot manage what is invisible.

Awareness

I'm a fan of Sherlock on Netflix. Sherlock Holmes possesses almost hyperbolic hyperawareness. He is constantly challenging others, especially Dr. Watson, to pay closer attention to their surroundings. "What do you see?" In every one of those incredible, rapid-fire crime scenes or character assessments, he imparts another extraordinary lesson on acute observation.

Writing will help us increase awareness. "What do you see?" "What do you think?" "How do you feel?" Think about this. If, before putting your head on your pillow at night, you would simply write down on one journal page where you saw God during your day, do you think you would be more aware of the blessings of His presence or less aware? Conversely, if you were to begin your day with a morning routine that included some writing about your day, how you were feeling, what you were hoping for, who you were going to see, what you were praying for in the lives of the people closest to you, do you think your awareness of God's activity around you, in you, and through you, would be heightened?

Many cannot answer the question about where they experienced God's presence throughout the day when it is posed to them. They cannot answer it because they have seldom stopped to consider Him. Writing is a tool that increases awareness.

Refining

Finding a way to express what you want to say in repeatable, understandable terms and writing it down will not only help you grasp a truth at a deeper, more profound level, it will help others understand what you are saying. I have a friend, Bob, who is always urging me to say it with fewer words. "Clearer!" "Shorter!" "Try again!"

He reminds me that Abraham Lincoln's Gettysburg Address is one of the most remembered speeches of all time. It lasted less than three minutes.

"On June 1, 1865, Senator Charles Sumner referred to the most famous speech ever given by President Abraham Lincoln. In his eulogy on the slain president, he called the Gettysburg Address a 'monumental act.' He said Lincoln was mistaken that 'the world will little note, nor long remember what we say here.' Rather, the Bostonian remarked, 'The world noted at once what he said, and will never cease to remember it. The battle itself was less important than the speech.'"[29]

One of the premier orators of the day, Edward Everett spoke before Lincoln gave his famous speech. His speech lasted over 2 hours. Bet you didn't know that!

Mr. Everett admired Lincoln's remarks and wrote to him the next day, "I should be glad, if I could flatter myself that I came as near to the central idea of the occasion, in two hours, as you did in two minutes."[30]

Brevity is not easy. It takes time and effort. As the old saying goes, "If I had more time, I would have written a shorter letter."

This writing cocktail (CAR) will help you discover your dream and give it life. Utilize these three steps and over time your dream will stick in your heart and in the minds of others.

Write then.

And, to write, you need to write.

There is a resistance to writing. The resistance was strong in me when I began to write. I suppose one of the reasons that resistance to writing is so strong is because of the clarity, awareness and refining that it delivers. There are times we don't like what we see. There are times we don't want to act on what we have come to understand.

29 Abraham Linclon, *The Gettysburg Address*, (Abraham Linclon Online), http://www.abrahamlincolnonline.org/lincoln/speeches/gettysburg.htm.
30 Ted Widmer, *The Other Gettysburg Address*, (The New York Times, Nov. 19, 2013), https://opinionator.blogs.nytimes.com/2013/11/19/the-other-gettysburg-address/.

The resistance is strong. The blessing is stronger still.

My resistance to writing persists. I still say things like:

"I'll get to it later."

"No one will benefit from what I have to say."

"I've got nothing. I'm dry."

"After the sermon, the articles, the letters, the website copy, the course introduction, the class, I've got nothing left!"

That's when I need the discipline to recall the writing promises that I outlined at the beginning of this lesson. Refer to them. Post them. Remember them.

And then, with that hope, begin writing. Even, and especially, when there seems that there is nothing to write about. In those moments I apply the 5-minute rule.

5-Minute Rule

"The 5-minute rule is a cognitive behavioral therapy technique for procrastination in which you set a goal of doing whatever it is you would otherwise avoid, but only do it for five minutes. If after five minutes it's so horrible that you have to stop, you are free to do so. Mission accomplished. Done."[31]

---

31 Andrea Bonior, *How Do You Stop Procrastinating? Use This 5-minute Rule,* (Huffington Post, July 5, 2014), https://www.huffingtonpost.com/andrea-bonior/how-do-you-stop-procrasti_b_5253087.html.

Three Things That Have Helped Me, and Will Help You Write

1. Seek a writing accountability partner who will check in on your writing progress.
2. Write only for yourself.
3. Read.

God gives you voice. He gives you insight. He is with you. He is guiding you. He shows you so much. Your insight blesses others. Don't keep it to yourself.

One final caveat: Sometimes we're not sure what exactly is going on in our heads until we commit thought to paper or screen. If you should choose to NOT share your thoughts with others, at least share them with yourself.

TRY THIS

If you don't enjoy writing, and you usually resist it or put it off, try applying the "5 minute" rule. For five minutes every day spend time writing. Set a timer and just write for five minutes. Or try it three times a week for five minutes. See if you are surprised by the gifts that are delivered as you write.

If you enjoy writing, keep it up!

Important Messages
Need to Be Repeated

For your dream to stick, it needs to be repeated so that it sticks with an audience and turns them into dream-supporters.

In the church world, the pressure is on to produce dynamic messages week after week. One preacher I know said, "The formula for a successful church is pretty easy. Great preaching + great music. Pretty simple." Yikes! I almost fell over in disbelief.

During my six-month sabbatical I did not miss preaching, even though I believe communication is my calling The pressure of delivering weekly, one-way proclamations had taken its toll on this preacher. I wouldn't call it hard work. Many times, however, it feels like unproductive work. I desperately want the dream to take root in every single person who hears it. Don't all dreamers want this? I can't think of any dreamer who set out on the pursuit because they wanted to go it alone.

God still has use of this gift he bestowed upon me. In my pursuit of great preaching, I am driven by the desire for transformational communication. After all, isn't that the goal of our preaching? Isn't this what "great preaching" is, or rather, should be? To communicate and inspire transformation in the lives of our listeners? The incarnation was not merely about sending Jesus to preach. He came to communicate. The way, the truth, the life. There is a place for proclamation. But we want the message to stick.

I get more enthusiastic thinking about "dripping" a message than I do "preaching" one. Drip. Drip. Drip. Here. There. Again. In one setting or another. Doesn't matter where. Formal settings and informal, planned and spontaneous, staged environments and unexpected conversations.

It doesn't take long for us to forget. We need reminders. Constantly. Like that drippy faucet. Until it finally sinks in, takes hold. It's as true for me as it for anyone else! That is, as long as we actually want the message to sink in.

Is our goal in preaching transmission or transformation? If we preachers are content to simply perform and proclaim, then it is possible that His message of truth may not land, will not take root. But, if we take interest in seeing the truth transform lives as evidenced by new life-sustaining behaviors then bit by bit, drip by drip, here, there, and everywhere we will see our influence.

This lesson is not just for preachers, by the way. Any one who dreams will eventually have a need to communicate that dream to someone. And dream communication is a complicated matter. Getting up on a platform and speaking to a crowd does not guarantee that it will stick. This is even true for those who make a habit of getting up on platforms and speaking to crowds. Your message, your dream will gain support in direct correlation to how well you heed this lesson.

Dreams gain momentum and support only when the dream's core message sticks. That dream sticks because it has been repeated over and over again. Different forums, different environments, different times. Different metaphors. Different descriptions, different constructions.

Perhaps one of the most important benefits of living out this lesson, and the reason it is in the Dream Spark part of this book, is that the more you describe your dream, the more it will stick for you. You will gain confidence. You will discover new ways of expressing it. You will uncover exciting new perspectives that bring more brilliance and depth to it.

TRY THIS

So, here's an exercise for dreamers who want to share their message. This will work for anyone who has a dream/message to share.

What is it that you really want to have sink in this week? Name it. Briefly. Now, look at your calendar for the week. Identify three potential message-dripping opportunities and decide how to use them. Lunch with a board member? Accountability time with a friend? Your weekly podcast or email to the congregation? Coffee with your daughter? Neighborhood get-together with your neighbors? Information session at church? Congregational meeting? Writing a piece for the church's monthly newsletter article? These are just a few of the things on my plate this week. How might I drip the message in a few of these opportunities? What do you notice from your list? Any creative message-dripping ideas pop up for you? Go for it.

The End of the Story Reads, "And He Lived Happily Ever After."

This popular phrase is more than a fairy tale ending. It is an attitudinal mantra that is available to you. It brings confidence and peace in the midst of your dream story. And, I believe, a perfect segue between the two parts of this book. Snuck in between a Dream Spark and a Realization Strategy it strikes a chord "And he lived happily ever after…"

My friend, Ron Goodsman, battled multiple myeloma for more than 15 years. In one of the last conversations I had with him he reminded me how the story ends. He was always doing that! This time, however, he was talking about his own end. Usually he was helping me redirect my thoughts in the middle of some struggle. But this time I think he was reminding himself.

"And he lived happily ever after…"

This morning, as I write this, I am thinking about the funeral I will be attending in a few hours. Last night I attended the visitation. My wife Amy and I stood in line for over four hours to pay our respects. The young man who died had just turned 21 years old. I wonder how many of the people who are grieving have someone to remind them how the story ends?

"And he lived happily ever after..."

On one of the tables in the high school gymnasium amid all of the photos of Will and his family and all of his accomplishments on the basketball court, a baptismal candle stood simply and unceremoniously. Next to it was a prayer rolled up like a scroll. What a beautiful and powerful prayer prayed for Will on his baptism day.

"And he lived happily ever after..."

Next to Pastor Goodsman's reading chair in his home in Clinton, Iowa hung this plaque. Simply and unceremoniously, it had called his attention back to the truth. A simple printout of a hymn was cut and pasted on a plaque.

> *My faith looks up to thee, thou Lamb of Calvary,*
> *Savior Divine*
> *Now hear me while I pray; take all my guilt away,*
> *Oh, let me from this day be wholly Thine.*
>
> *May thy rich grace impart, strength to my fainting*
> *heart, My zeal inspire!*
> *As thou hast died for me, oh may my love for thee,*
> *Pure, warm, and changeless be, a living fire!*
>
> *While life's dark maze I tread and grief around me*
> *spread, Be thou my guide*
> *Bid darkness turn to day, wipe sorrows' tears away,*
> *Nor let me ever stray from thee aside*

When ends life's transient dream, when death's cold,
sullen stream shall o'er me roll.
Blest Savior then in love, fear, and distrust remove,
Oh, bear me safe above, a ransomed soul! [32]

That plaque hangs next to that chair still. In my home. Simply and unceremoniously it reminds me.

My faith looks up to thee, thou Lamb of Calvary,
Savior Divine
Now hear me while I pray; take all my guilt away,
Oh, let me from this day be wholly Thine...

"And he lived happily ever after..."

May thy rich grace impart, strength to my fainting
heart, My zeal inspire!
As thou hast died for me, oh may my love for thee,
Pure, warm, and changeless be, a living fire!

"And he lived happily ever after..."

While life's dark maze I tread and grief around me
spread, Be thou my guide
Bid darkness turn to day, wipe sorrows' tears away,
Nor let me ever stray from thee aside

"And he lived happily ever after..."

32 Ray Palmer, *My Faith Looks Up to Thee,* (St. Louis: Concordia Publishing House, 1941), The Lutheran Hymnal #394.

When ends life's transient dream, when death's cold,
sullen stream shall o'er me roll.
Blest Savior then in love, fear, and distrust remove,
Oh, bear me safe above, a ransomed soul!

"And he lived happily ever after..."

In the middle of our sin and its guilt-producing effects.

"And he lived happily ever after..."

In the middle of the all-consuming pace of our lives, exhausted and weary.

"And he lived happily ever after..."

In the middle of the confusing twists and turns of our days, unable to clearly discern our next step.

"And he lived happily ever after..."

And, finally, in the midst of death reminding us of the fragility and transient nature of this existence.

"And he lived happily ever after..."

At the end of the pursuit of your dream this truth stands. No matter how the dream turns out. Regardless of whether or not you achieve all you wanted or hoped to achieve.

"And he lived happily ever after..."

So, what if in the midst of the effort to chase after that dream you could remember…

"And he lived happily ever after…"

As you consider your dream, this simple phrase is the reason we can say "Fear not. Dream Big." You can't fail. With Jesus this end is inevitable.

"And he lived happily ever after…"

TRY THIS

"And he lived happily ever after…"

How do you need this reminder today? How will you remember it?

Hold on. Grab on. Determine to cling to it. At all costs, don't let go.

PART 2

Realization Strategies

Strategies

Steps taken to pursue an inspired vision

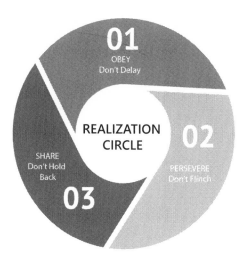

Morning Has Broken.
Sit Awhile with Your Creator

I think Cat Stevens (or Yusef, if you prefer) had it right: "morning has broken, like the first morning." Every morning takes us back to the first morning and a relationship with the Creator that is purified and refreshed.

The day is best begun by accepting an invitation from the Master of ALL things to spend some unhurried, undistracted time with Him. Accept the invitation and you will enjoy the provisions of that day.

Seek FIRST the Kingdom of God...and all these things will be added... (to your day)... (Matthew 6:33).

Anxiety-producing compulsions are quieted in the Master's presence. The searching, striving, and struggling to get daily provision is stilled in His presence because He is the Provider of all of it. Sure, you can get stuff without Him. But at what cost? Anxiety. Stress. Busyness.

It is possible to get all the stuff without the angst. IN HIS PRESENCE at the beginning of every day.

So, in this regard, here's a prescription for the realization of your God-sparked dream.

Begin each day with Him by remembering your...**ABC's**

Acknowledge that He is the Provider, that what we receive is simply a gift from the Author of Life. From start to finish, the day is His. By beginning the day with Him, you *proclaim* that He is the One who will give you everything you need. "Give us today our *daily* bread."

Believe that He has bestowed promise upon this particular day.. He has something to speak to you on THIS day. That promise is personal and it is specific. Receive it. Beginning this day with Him provides *promise* for THIS day.

Commit your day to His purpose. This commitment gets us outside of ourselves and reminds us that THIS day has been given to us for a purpose greater than our own pursuit. Beginning this day with Him *prioritizes* His mission.

In the Old Testament book of Exodus (Chapter 16), there is a perfect illustration of this truth. God wanted to teach the children of Israel to honor Him daily while they were in the wilderness so that they would live out the ABC's in the promised land. God provided food enough for every day. Bread every morning. Meat every evening. God's people were to gather enough for their family each day. No storing up. No hoarding. Each day enough given and received, but just for that day. It's not difficult to recognize Israel's struggle to integrate this rhythm, *praise each day, receive each day.* We can identify with the struggle all too well.

It's in our nature to want to provide for ourselves. So, beginning each day with this act of acknowledging that ultimately we rely on Providence, not ourselves, is not as easy as it sounds. Instead of sitting with our Provider, we'll want to get to work. Answer email. Plan our day. Check Facebook. Jump in the shower. Take on the day.

Why not start by entrusting the day to God? Give it a try. I dare ya.

TRY THIS

Begin tomorrow by waking up and saying: "This is your day, Lord."

Will you accept the challenge? Will you entrust your day to God?

Try out the ABC rhythm:

Acknowledge:

Proclaim that God is the provider of all that you have. Praise Him for who He is. Compile a list of God's attributes and focus on a different one each day. (Provider, Shepherd, King of kings, Potentate, Healer, etc.)

Believe:

The **Promise** for this day is a specific promise for you. It is also for THIS DAY. Use your calendar to visualize your day. What promise will you receive *today*? Believe that God is with you each moment of this day. He promises to never leave you or forsake you. He promises to guide you and direct your steps. Thank him for the promises and believe that they are true for you.

Commit:

Surrender the day to God. Commit your thoughts, actions, attitudes and schedule to him. Ask him to direct your steps. **Prioritizing** your day by putting Him first, keeps His mission in front of you, it makes your day about Him and not you.

Try the ABC rhythm for one week.

What was it like? Did you notice anything different about yourself?

Try it again for another week if it helped you in any way.

LESSON 2

Get in Rhythm with Your Priorities, Starting with Jesus

On account of my forgetfulness, my distracted nature, and my open rebellion, I need to build into my daily existence routines that direct me back to the presence and leadership of Jesus as discussed in Lesson 9. Fortunately, there are a number of these routines. I refer to them as "rhythms" because the intention is to incorporate them so deeply into my everyday life that they become second nature, like another heartbeat. The thing is, they don't come from fortune, though; they come from Providence. They originate and emanate from God. They are His gifts to us. They redirect and remind.

There is a flow to your day. You have grown accustomed to it over time. You carry out some of it automatically, without much thought. These rhythms allow you to preserve much needed brain power for the decisions that will need to be made throughout your day. You only have so much space for decisions each day.

This flow can be adapted as you live your life. In fact, you have already adapted it many times. There are things you do in your daily rhythms today that you did not do a year ago. There are also things you did 5 years ago that you are not doing today.

What I am suggesting here is for you to be very intentional about including daily rhythms that help you redirect your heart and mind to the One who gave you all that you have. Your dream will not be disappointed. Ok, so how will you find time for some much needed refreshment and realignment? There are moments as you begin, moments in the middle, and moments at the end of your day that are perfectly suited for a Divine intermission. Schedule it. Build it in. Live it out. Let it become second nature.

Here are some personal examples that I have included through the years:

Listening Prayer – sitting in silence in order to listen to God. What is He asking you to do in that moment? Any clarity from Him on what your next move should be? When it comes across loud and clear, get up, go and do it.

Lectio Divina ("Divine Reading") – this Benedictine contemplative practice allows you to listen deeply with your ear to the heart of a passage of Scripture as it is read to you out loud multiple times in order to discern what God is saying to you in that moment. Phrases or words will emerge that are really speaking to you in that moment. This way of reading the Scriptures is almost like having a conversation with God.

1 @ 1-Send a text to yourself or have a friend check in with you via text at 1 p.m. (or anytime you prefer) every day to remind you to drop everything you are doing and pray, breathe, read a scripture passage.

Memorizing Scripture – write out a passage for the week and carry it with you in a 3x5 card, or in a note on your phone and pull it out throughout the day in order to read it, repeat it so that it sticks in your memory.

Prayer Walking – this rhythm could have a double benefit. It will get you up and out of your office chair and on the move. If you're going to be walking anyway, why not walk and pray. Around your neighborhood, or in your office building, pray onsite with insight.

Read Written Prayers – morning, midday, evening, or night, stop what you are doing for a brief prayer interlude. Pick up your favorite prayer book and read the prayers. Pray them to God. Here are a couple of my favorites:

- Diary of Private Prayer[33]
- Everyday Prayers[34]

Daily Examen – before you go to bed, stop and intentionally reflect on your day. Like rummaging through your day looking for God, this ancient spiritual discipline (hence, the spelling of "Examen") can help increase your awareness of God's movement in your life so that you are better able to join Him in it. Daily Examen consists of two foundational questions and three steps. I would encourage you to write your responses in a journal.

33 John Baillie, *A Diary of Private Prayer*, (New York: Scribner, 2014).
34 Scotty Smith, *Everyday Prayers: 365 Days to a Gospel-Centered Faith*, (Grand Rapids: Baker, 2011).

Ask the two questions:

1. God, where have I felt your presence, seen your face, heard your Word this day?
2. God, where have I ignored you, run from you, perhaps even rejected you this day?

Then, take some time to speak with God about what you discovered.

"God, I thank you for the times this day we have been together and worked together… "(pray specifically as you reflect on your answers above.)

"God, I am sorry for the ways that I have offended you by what I have done or what I did not do…" (pray specifically as you reflect on your answers above.)

Finally, before you go to sleep pray for your day tomorrow.

"God, I ask that you draw me ever closer to you this day and tomorrow so that I may recognize your presence more clearly. God, you are the God of my life—thank you."

Journal Written Prayers: Stop whatever you are doing and write out a prayer to God.

Sit in Silence and Envision Sitting With Jesus and Talking to Him: Stop whatever you are doing and talk to Jesus about your day. What's happened so far? What is coming up? How are you doing? What thoughts are consuming you? What are you happy about?

Post a Scripture Passage on Facebook: Drop a note to the world and share the passage that has been on your mind. This can be another helpful way to memorize scripture.

Sing a Hymn: Pull out your favorite hymn book and sing a favorite hymn. Try out a new one if you so desire.

Play a Favorite Spotify Playlist: Create a few playlists of your current favorite songs/hymns that help you fix your eyes on Jesus. Plug and play throughout your day.

Commit to a Weekly Review: Practice Reflect and Reset. Pick a time and day of the week for this practice. Who could you ask to hold you capable? A simple text message: Did you Reflect and Reset last night?

Reflect:

- What were the highlights of the past week?
- What are you thankful for?
- What are you particularly proud that you accomplished?
- Where did you see God in your work last week?
- Where did you see the fruit of your labors?
- Based on last week's experience, what should you do more of? Less of?
- Where did you waste time?
- What didn't work out so well?

Pick three questions and answer them for one week. Journal your answers. Try again for another week. You may want to try different questions to answer from the list or others you have thought of, yourself.

Reset:

Plan your week!

Look through your long list of to-dos. Prioritize the list. And place that list on your daily calendar. I would suggest no more than 3 big to-dos per day.

Pay attention to the meetings and recurring events during your week.

Block out bigger chunks of time for bigger projects.

Leave space to breathe. In fact, schedule it. Don't pack your schedule so full.

Where is the realization of your dream on your calendar? Reserve some time and breath to keep the embers glowing.

One of the keys to incorporating these rhythms into our lives is to learn to approach this with a loose grip. Don't be so legalistic and regimented with your faith. It's a relationship. None of these rhythms need be set in concrete. You have the power to adapt as you go. Look at this as a grand experiment. Try out some things. If one doesn't fit, try another. Ask others who have daily rhythms with Jesus to share with you what they have tried through the years. Try out their ideas. Custom-fit them. Make them your own.

By similar means, you can use God-given patterns to organize your life.

1. DAILY (rotational)
2. WEEKLY (sabbath)
3. MONTHLY (lunar)
4. QUARTERLY (seasonal)
5. YEARLY (orbital)

Within each of these five basic units, which practices, regimens, and routines can you implement that would help align your values and your actions? (Without asserting this intentionality, you are more likely to be driven by the pace of life and the expectations of others. And God designed you to be led not driven.)

What is something(s) you want to do every day?

Every week?

Every month?

Every quarter?

Every year?

Of all the things you should do, what MUST you do? I'm talking non-negotiables, your no-exception priorities. Write them down somewhere prominent. Write them in your planner. I'm talking about the important things, not just the urgent things. These are the priorities that preserve your life, your thinking, your creativity, your energy, your sanity.

Don't allow ANYTHING to get in the way. Review these priorities relentlessly. If you are not keeping your commitment to one of them, ask yourself again if it is a non-negotiable. If it is, renew your commitment. If it isn't, drop it or change it. Determine to make sure that these no-exception priorities will be accomplished.

You need to think about these non-negotiables in terms of your professional life, your relational life, your spiritual life, and your physical/emotional life. Here's a quick, partial list of some of mine to get you thinking:

- Exercise
- Time with Amy
- Time with my girls
- Scripture
- Reading
- Writing
- Retreats Alone
- Sleep
- Healthy Eating

TRY THIS

What daily rhythm do you have in place that helps you follow Jesus?

What daily rhythm would you like to try?

Who could you ask to help you follow through on your plan, or participate with you?

Now it's your turn to list your non-negotiables. Go ahead and just brain dump a list of all the things you want to do, that you must do to be healthy in pursuit of your dream.

Then, when you are ready, turn the page.

	Professional	Relational	Spiritual	Physical
DAILY Rotational				
WEEKLY Sabbath				
MONTHLY Lunar				
QUARTERLY Seasonal				
YEARLY Orbital				

LESSON 3

With God's Help I Can
Control My Thinking

You are not victim to your thoughts. You are not helpless to endure whatever randomness enters your mind. You are not defenseless against an onslaught of debilitating self-talk. You are not a feeble-minded person. You have been created in the image of God. He has given you the capacity to manage your thoughts. Apply that truth to your thought life. You can make every thought captive to Christ. God would never instruct you to do something that you do not have the capacity to do. That's just cruel. Read 2 Corinthians 10:5 and ruthlessly apply Paul's words to this issue of managing your thoughts.

So many times I have thought I was shackled by my thoughts. Under their chirping assault, I just endured and tried to carry on. Many of my thoughts are not helpful. They are actually impediments. But, "God has spoken from His sanctuary." (New International Version, Psalm 60:6)

Here's the source of the problem: too much self-focus untempered by God-focus. One of the main culprits in our thought life is that we spend way too much energy thinking about ourselves. Isn't this the ultimate result of sin? Self-awareness is good. Self-focus, to the exclusion of all else, is deadly. "O Lord, our hearts are restless until they find their rest in Thee."[35]

Your thinking can be your worst enemy. Your thought life can be the greatest barrier to the realization of your dream. One must learn to rest as you realize.

How do we rest? Not rest in our body, per se, but rest in our thoughts. Here are some practices I have found life-giving, that is, IF I actually PRACTICE them. I can't merely learn about them. I need to develop habits from them.

With God's help I can control my thinking by...

Recalling

Daily Examen. Rummage through your day and ask:

"Where did I notice you today, Lord, and join you?"

"Where did I notice you today, Lord, and not join you?"

If your dream has a Divine Spark, then the Lord will certainly be leading you, providing for you, encouraging you in your next steps. The key question for us is, Will we follow His lead?

---

35 St. Augustine, *Confessions* I.1.

Repeating

Speak truth, God's truth, out loud each time that self-defeating voice pops into your head. *"Give us aid against the enemy for human help is worthless. With God we gain victory, and He will trample down our enemies."* *(New International Version, Psalm 60:11-12)*

It is helpful to collect a few go-to phrases that you can repeat to yourself in moments of doubt. Scripture, lines of hymns or poetry, rhythmic one-liners, are great sources of inspiration. Ask others to help you brainstorm a list. Pick your favorites. Memorize them. Then, repeat them when that self-defeating voice pops into your head.

Rejoicing

If you truly believed that God inhabits the praise of His people, how would it change your behavior? My guess would be that you would celebrate a whole lot more than you do now! Dreamers tend to keep pushing forward. On to the next task. Dissatisfaction with the status quo pushes us forward. It is incumbent upon us dreamers that we pause and build celebration into our days. Don't skip days. And if you happen to miss a day, please don't miss weeks. Build it into your rhythms to celebrate! You are making progress. God is blessing your pursuit. He is with you as you execute your dream.

Relaxing

Learn to breathe. Learn to be mindful. Train your mind to acknowledge the plaguing thoughts and then let them go on by.

Releasing

Draw a circle that fills your page. Now, draw a circle within that circle, one that is half the diameter. Now, within the space BETWEEN the two circles write all the things in the situation you are thinking about that you cannot control. Now, inside the inner circle write out the things you can control. Refocus your energy on the inner circle. Black out the other stuff. Seriously, for real, black it out. Or cut it out. Take scissors and trim all that excess stuff off the page. Then, use the inner circle to plan how you will do something about what you CAN control. Fix your attention on that. So much of life is beyond our control. But there is still more than enough within our control to occupy us for the rest of our days.

Is there anything from this lesson that you are willing to try? What do you have to lose? Maybe your inhibiting thoughts? Maybe your distracted mind? Wouldn't that be nice? Just a thought.

TRY THIS

Recalling   Repeating   Rejoicing
Relaxing   Releasing

Which one of these practices grabs your heart right now? Which one would you like to try this week? Go ahead and just give it a try.

LESSON 4

Chase the Truth.
Don't Follow the Feeling

I need to discipline my mind to do this.

As a Type Four on the Enneagram I have spent a lifetime following my feelings in any given situation. It has come naturally to me to interpret situations predominantly on the basis of my feelings. (For more information on Type Fours on Enneagram, see *Appendix*, p. 319.)

The important thing for me to remember is that it is a natural characteristic for me to interpret my feelings as fact automatically. It is not natural for me to step back and question the legitimacy of my feelings. It is vital that I do so, however. Here's why. Feelings are not facts. Situations are more than the emotions they stir up. I am more than my feelings.

This may be a challenge for you too as you pursue your dream. All kinds of emotions will well up within you as you march on. Here are a few thoughts on putting your emotions in their proper place in regard to your dream pursuit.

Investigate your emotional reactions.

I have found that writing down my feelings in a two-columned journal throughout the day allows me to assess them with greater clarity. I encourage you to do the same. Describe what you are feeling in the first column. Simply jot your feelings down. As they come, experience them. Recognize them. Don't wrestle with them or challenge them in the moment. Just acknowledge their reality. Then move on.

At the end of the day, fill in the second column. Search Scripture. Search your memory banks. Write down in the second column any additional thoughts, feelings, and considerations related to the emotional trigger and/or your emotional reaction next to the feelings you had written down earlier.

Emotional Reaction	Upon Further Reflection
This relationship pattern I am experiencing with _____ will never end. I am never going to be able to change it. I'm just beating my head against the wall!	I cannot control the pattern or _____'s response. I can control mine. What can I do differently next time? How can I change the dance?
I am so alone. I'm up against the world. No one understands. I feel completely abandoned.	God says, "I am with you always" (Matthew 28:20).

What methods do you use to test your feelings?

Tell yourself the truth.

What is YOUR source of truth? Where do you turn when your emotions threaten to disrupt your composure? What's the bedrock upon which you base your worldview? For me it is God's Word. Yet, how often do I search that source when confronted with an overwhelming feeling? Too often I derive truth from emotion instead of checking it against the objective truth of God. In those moments I am prioritizing subjective truth over objective truth. It's okay to have feelings. We shouldn't suppress them or deny them. But we should challenge them. Especially when they are having a negative effect on our psyche.

The key to accomplishing this is putting certain measures in place BEFORE the feelings arrive. If the Word of God is your source, you will be much better prepared to tell yourself the truth by having already familiarized yourself with that truth. It's kind of like a soldier in battle. The warrior has diligently prepared and practiced the skills necessary for battle BEFORE the battle begins. I remember, back when I was a college basketball player, practicing before a big game against a team that brought relentless full court pressure. We practiced all week, the five of us trying to get the ball down the court into the front court against eight teammates. When it came to the moment of truth, we were prepared.

What methods are you using to prepare right now so that when you need to, you can tell yourself the truth?

Train yourself.

Enneagram Type Fours need to learn how to tap into the pattern of healthy Type Ones...acting on objective principles, not subjective emotions. Often as a Four on the Enneagram I live through my feelings. I respond and act on the basis of my emotions. Emulating Type Ones in this regard, I shift from wallowing in my feelings to moving forward.

We must find strategies to put our feelings in their proper place. Feelings are deceptive. It is not that they are bad. In and of themselves, feelings have little meaning. It is our interpretation of them that is critical. Our interpretations of our feelings are not always rooted in truth. Fortunately, there are strategies you can employ to anchor yourself to the bedrock of truth. These strategies can distract us long enough so that our conditioned interpretations of our particular feelings pass by and give us a chance to deal with the situation as it is, not as it is after we project our emotions on it.

Dr. Andrea Bonior, a clinical psychologist, who teaches at Georgetown University and wrote the bestseller, *Psychology: Essential Thinkers, Classic Theories, and How They Inform Your World*, suggests seven such strategies for dealing with anxiety. Anxiety may not be an issue for you, but these strategies can help you avoid negative emotional interpretations. Two of my favorite from this post are *shifting your senses* and a *weighted blanket*. What does shifting the senses and a weighted blanket have to do with training yourself?

Here are a couple of quotes from Dr. Bonoir's post to consider:

Shift Your Senses

"Are there particular smells you like, visuals you find calming, or specific music that can snap you out of your swirling thoughts? Even a particularly beloved type of candy or gum — if savored and used to switch the focus to the here and now — can serve as a punctuation mark, a physical reminder to stop the thought cycle and just focus on the sensation you're experiencing right in this moment."

Weighted Blanket

"The firm pressure of a weighted blanket can bring about a feeling of safety and comfort. If you like the idea, but don't want to try that particular object, you might come up with your own way to feel cocooned — through a warm and soothing bath, being held by a partner, or enveloping yourself in a series of textures that feel soft and soothing."[36]

TRY THIS

In this lesson I mention two of the 7 ideas from Dr. Bonoir's Post.[37]

Which of the seven strategies do you like to try? Would you add any of your own to her list?

---

36 Andrea Bonior, *Seven In-the-Moment Tools to Lessen Anxiety: Here's what to do when you just can't shake it.,* (Psychology Today, Dec. 12, 2017), https://www.psychologytoday.com/blog/friendship-20/201712/seven-in-the-moment-tools-lessen-anxiety.
37 *ibid.*

Train Your Mind
via Your Mouth

Our thoughts bump around inside our heads until they are spoken and challenged. They cannot be considered and appraised without first being pulled out of the silence of interiority and brought into the light of day, into earshot. Not just speaking. Journaling, emailing, voice recording... You get the picture.

We train our minds via our mouths.

Silent self-talk will stick in the psyche if it goes unchallenged. Unchallenged, self-abasing self-talk over time, at the very least, disrupts the pursuit of dreams. At worst, destroys them. Think rust, mold, barnacles. There will always be obstacles in the realization phase of putting skin and bones to your dream. Inevitably, things will get in the way. Not all will go according to plan. In order to execute, you will need to learn how to adapt, and with learning of any kind comes frustration.

As you encounter these setbacks you learn more and more about yourself. Your response to adversity, failure, and confusion is revealing. You will also discover your level of discipline, determination and resolve to stay the course. And in this process of acquiring greater self-knowledge, you will have a lot of conversations in your head. If you are introspective at all, you will uncover a patterned narrative of self-talk.

Your pattern of self-talk may be different than mine. The same principle, however, applies to both of ours. You can train your mind by going public with your thoughts.

One of my patterned narratives is that I beat myself up for setbacks. I also speak poorly about myself when I stumble upon something that I need to learn. For some reason, I think I should know either everything or be able to figure it out in an instant when I don't know it. Even as I type this, I realize how silly that notion is. That's what I mean by *getting out of your head and expressing yourself.*

Allow me to get personal for a minute. In pursuit of MY dream it has become quite clear that I need to be kinder to myself. That kindness gets sparked by speaking my thoughts out loud and challenging them. There are so many things I can do in place of beating myself up. But do you see? I can neither learn those things nor implement them if I don't first make my thoughts visible and challengeable.

There is always a payoff for our persistent thoughts and the behaviors that follow. So, what is the payoff for beating yourself up? What is the reward for self-deprecating remarks? It's not so obvious. Dig deeper, however, and you may discover something. Stick with me here. There is a payoff, and we'll get there. Honest reflection can open the door to a new, life-transforming self-dialogue.

Replace the self-defeating comments with comments that reflect a greater, more generous understanding of yourself. Exchange the default pattern with a fresh, new thought. A counselor in my early days of ministry (as you can see, this pattern has been going on a long time) taught me to challenge negative thoughts and reaffirm the truth.

What's your patterned self-talk?

Our mantras seem to have become enmeshed in the fabric of our souls. But what if I told you that our mantras are old and tired and that it's time to move on? What if I said, it's time to shed them, retire them because they aren't doing you any favors!

But, they fit so nicely. They're so comfortable. Like a comfortable pair of jeans, they just fit better. And there it is. There is something we *crave* about our self-defeating self-talk. There is a sense of normalcy. We are used to it. And there is the payoff: *familiarity*.

You are a dream-maker, though. That is your true identity. God has seen to it. He created and redeemed you to bless the world with your dream. So shed the destructive self-talk and move on in your pursuit.

TRY THIS

If you can step outside of our experience for a moment and look at your current circumstance from an outsider's perspective, you might get a more accurate view.

How is your self-talk working for you?

Have you glimpsed different results when you have trained your mind via your mouth?

What did that look like? What did that feel like?

What if you did more of that and less of your normal self-talk?

What narrative are you ready to change?

Write down that narrative. How would you describe it?

For one week take some time at the end of each day and reflect on thoughts that went unchallenged. Divide the paper into two columns. One for "thoughts" and the other for "Truth." Go back through your day and write out all of the unchallenged thoughts you allowed to rumble through your noggin. Then write out the truth in the other column. Practicing this discipline over time will help you get out of your head and express yourself more clearly.

Here is an example from my life to get you thinking.

Thought: I'm so stupid. I should be able to figure this out!

Truth: I am not stupid. I am quite intelligent. There will always be unknowns that will need to be figured out in learning a new skill. This is a natural part of the process.

Live Life Like You Button a Shirt

It is a ridiculous notion to put on a dress shirt and button it from the bottom up. You align the shirt from the top down. And then you button, one at a time, working your way down.

We would be better living our days as we button our shirt, with first things first. The most important things first. Start off your day by tackling the items that are highest priority. Like the rock and sand in the jar illustration. First rocks, then sand.

Living your day like you button a shirt…

…keeps you from missing tasks.

Have you ever buttoned a shirt in a hurry and missed buttons? Start in the middle or from the bottom and you will. It's too easy to miss buttons when the shirt isn't properly aligned from top to bottom.

If you don't start at the top, your day will be consumed with whatever contingencies arise and you will miss buttons. You will miss the important items.

...helps you distinguish essential tasks from the extraneous

With most dress shirts there are extra buttons at the bottom. Does anyone know what purpose these serve? Are they replacements for real buttons? I think they are, though I can't recall ever using them. If you were to use them to replace a button, how would you ever get them off? Someone just introduced me to a seam ripper. Who knew?

The extra button at the bottom of the shirt isn't actually meant to be buttoned. Knowing which is the actual button and which is the extra is critical! The buttons that need to be buttoned get buttoned.

Starting with first things first will ensure that you accomplish all of the items you NEED to accomplish. Leave the "extra" things alone. If you are particularly effective that day, you can always deal with the extra things afterward, if you have time.

This may sound like a simple lesson. Well, it is. Yet, how often do we push off the essential task in our day, despite knowing how essential it is! The essential tasks are the ones that will help you best execute that dream. Make progress every day on your dream. If you miss a day, just make sure it doesn't turn into a week. Pick yourself up and get started again today.

You have named your dream. Figure out what you need to accomplish in the next couple of weeks to move toward it. Make progress. Schedule the essentials. Leave the extras alone.

Go public with your dream. Risk sharing it. Tell some people about it. Write it out. Post it. Then articulate your One-year goal. Then, working backwards, put a line in the sand for 90 days out. This will help you determine what your next essential steps will be in realizing your dream. Pick out that button-down and put it on with confidence. Your dream will thank you!

TRY THIS

What will you do to remember to start with the top button?

Make a list of all the things you need to do today. Now go back over the list and mark those that are essential for TODAY.

How will you prioritize the list of essentials?

Overcome Procrastination with This Simple Fix

I understand two things. One, I am prone to distraction. Two, that doesn't exactly set me apart from others. In this age of information overload, there are more ways to distract ourselves than ever before.

I am coming to understand that many of my distractions are delays. I delay accomplishing the task in front of me because I don't want to do it. I avoid another because I don't think I'm good at it. Often the "it" just needs to get done, however.

When I procrastinate I tell myself I am not a good time manager, that I'm lazy. *If I just had more willpower..!* Delaying is an avoidance strategy. Instead of just doing it, I will frequently replace that task with something that gives me a mood boost.

Doesn't sound so irrational, does it?

Instead of knocking out that budget review, I will work on my website. In lieu of unpacking after my trip, I will surf the web looking for that item I have convinced myself that I need. Then, on top of not completing the task and getting it out of the way, I heap on great gobs of guilt with the negative self-talk. It is a cycle, and it's the exact opposite of productive. Unfortunately, I'm learning that this pattern is a pretty common one. There is even a free podcast devoted to procrastination! For these moments of procrastination, I have discovered a little trick that actually works. It takes a certain amount of discipline and self-coaching to initiate the trick, and that is why I think it is such a great strategy for procrastination. One of the biggest challenges for procrastinators is to get started. This trick tackles that challenge brilliantly. It gets you to drop the end-results thinking and just get started by taking the next step.

It's called the five-minute rule. Pick a task that you have been avoiding and commit yourself to get after it for five minutes. Just get started. That's so much more palatable than "Just Do It" (NIKE's old tagline). *Just start.*

"What can I possibly get done in five minutes?" you ask yourself. But that is the procrastinator talking, the voice that would at this very moment lobby for doing nothing rather than doing anything at all. Are you going to listen to that voice? Don't. So let's ask again: What can you get done in five minutes? Five minutes more work than you would have done otherwise, and often the hardest part of all."[38]

Dr. Bonior, who has worked for years in the area of Cognitive Behavior Therapy, insists that in order for this to work well, you will need to commit to just the five minutes and then stop. You will have experienced some movement forward and felt good about that, which will leave you more willing to take on another five-minute sprint the following day. Or, you may have accomplished that simple

38 Bonior, *How Do You Stop Procrastinating? Use This 5-Minute Rule,* (Huffington Post, July 5, 2014).

task in the five minutes that you allotted. It may not have been so big and scary after all.

"So, just tell yourself you can do five minutes. You absolutely can. It's not nearly as scary as an hour or an all-nighter. Whether it's writing that first paragraph or just ordering the book that you're supposed to be reading, that first step truly begins the bulk of the progress in getting there."[39]

Give it a shot today when you notice the delay. When you start to pick up on your pattern of avoidance, or your self-soothing replacement activity taking over, stop and say: "Alright, alright already. I'll get started for five minutes."

TRY THIS

Put yourself on the clock. Get out your phone, initiate your timer for five minutes, and get started.

---

39 *ibid.*

LESSON 8

Space Matters

We are controlled by outside influences, some for good, some for ill. Distractions move us off target. Being off target over time results in loss of purpose and confused identity.

Surrounded by clutter, we are ineffective. Clutter distracts. Clutter blurs. Soft focus reduces power, and we need all the power we can muster to make any real impact.

The latest psychological research on clutter suggests a connection between physical and mental clutter, which contributes to a loss of positive self-identity, reduced cognition, even unhealthy eating!

The space I'm talking about is physical space AND mental space. Cluttered with stuff. Cluttered with thoughts. Same results.

Physical clutter can hinder your ability to stay on track because excessive visual stimuli in your physical space compete for your attention. Furthermore, isn't it stressful to live in a space that you know must be cleaned and put into order at some point, the prospect of all that extra work hanging over your head?

Similarly, mental clutter makes it much more difficult to filter out irrelevant information. Thoughts competing for your attention jumble your thinking.

So, check this out. Scrolling through an article on the psychology of clutter, I was suddenly distracted by pop-up ads. Suddenly vying for my attention were pictures of products and offers from companies I have purchased from in the past. I clicked on the ads! Now, I was running down a new rabbit hole. My focus was in a completely different and unproductive spot. I just lost, at least, 20 minutes window shopping online. That's not even taking into consideration the extra time it took me to get back on track once I returned to the work I was supposed to be doing.

"Mehmood Hanif, a marketing strategist who represents Bad Ad Johnny, estimates that the average Internet user is served 11,250 ads per month, which he bases on the number of times the software blocks a banner or pop-up."[40] Yikes!

As I sit here writing this lesson there are no fewer than 15 different books scattered about the space next to where I am sitting. Three open journals on my desk. Two shirts, a belt, and a pair of shoes from a recent road trip that haven't yet found their way back into the closet. There are two Amazon boxes. One opened that should be in the recycle bin by now. The other unopened. I have notes written on post-its on the stand next to the chair where I am sitting. At a

40 Christopher Elliott, *Yes, There Are Too Many Ads Online. Yes, You Can Stop Them. Here's How.* (Huffington Post, Feb. 9, 2017), https://www.huffingtonpost.com/entry/yes-there-are-too-many-ads-online-yes-you-can-stop_us_589b888de4b02bbb1816c297.

glance, I am reminded of what I need to bring to a Leadership Board meeting later this week.

I have a problem.

If I am to remain diligently focused on executing my dream I will need a clutter-reducing strategy. How will I eliminate the physical clutter? How will I eliminate the mental clutter and focus on one thing at a time?

1. Clear Your Inbox
2. Clear Your Desk
3. Plan your day the day before.
4. Use an Ad-Free Browser or an Add-eliminating plug-in App. This will help you execute your own personal ad-stopping online reading experience. This post from the Huffington Post[41] gives you a few options to help you begin to develop your own plan. I have used Min Browser,[42] and AdBlock Plus.[43]
5. Write down your random thoughts. Write down your thoughts in a notebook so a) you won't forget them, and b) you can review them later and stop fixating on them in the present. Schedule space to come back later and review the list.
6. Pomodoro Technique:[44] work at one thing in front of you for 25 minutes.

41 *ibid.*
42 *Min Browser,* https://minbrowser.github.io/min/.
43 *AdBlock Plus,* https://adblockplus.org/.
44 *Pomodoro Technique,* https://francescocirillo.com/pages/pomodoro-technique.

Do any of these ideas sound interesting enough for you to try? Pick one idea and try it. Don't try to implement all of these at once. Master one and then move on. And remember, it is not enough to know that you need to do these things to reduce clutter. You will need to be relentless in maintaining the discipline. Or, like me, the clutter will creep back in. And when it does, because it eventually will, avoid beating yourself up. Instead, go back and do what you have done in the past that has worked. Try again. You are not a victim to your cluttering ways! You can act. Today. Right now.

TRY THIS

Take an inventory of your space. Look around you right now. What do you notice?

What can you do to declutter your physical space that you work in?

Take an inventory of your brain. Get a piece of paper and write down all the things you are thinking about. What do you notice?

How can you begin to declutter your mind?

Which one of the five strategies that were shared do you want to try?

Sound Sleep Matters

If you suspect that you have an undiagnosed sleep issue, please consider contacting a sleep professional and getting a consultation or sleep test. This is no small matter. The risks of untreated sleep issues are significant. The realization strategies in this part of the book will be of little help. If you do have an undiagnosed sleep disorder, you probably require greater assistance than this chapter provides.

I know this from personal experience.

After years of cajoling from my dear wife, Amy, who has lived with the distinct honor of nudging me every night when I stop breathing, I finally bowed to her insistence and took a sleep test. She, along with her brother and father, promised that "it would change my life."

Sleep apnea is a sleep disorder that interrupts your breathing while sleeping. This enemy of sleep not only disrupts sound sleep, it also impacts the body's access to much needed oxygen for recovery. It can lead to heart disease as well. Surgery is an option, but for my treatment I have chosen to use a CPAP, a machine that throughout the night pushes air through your nose and/or mouth, thereby providing a steady flow of oxygen to your lungs.

Since that sleep test and subsequent diagnosis, I have learned much about the importance of sleep. As my sleep disorder awareness has expanded so has my related vocabulary. Sleep debt, insomnia, acid reflux, alcohol consumption, bruxism (the grinding of teeth in one's sleep), caffeine, chocolate, daytime and nighttime sleep hygiene, naps, light exposure, waking routine, use of electronics, bedtime routine, room temperature, noise, exercise, sleep quality, and sleep quantity.

I've tried sleep aids of all kinds. Yoga. Meditation. Natural Melatonin. Over-the-counter sleep medication.

I am not going to spend any time here attempting to convince you why sound sleep matters. If you aren't already convinced, there are plenty of easily available scientific studies that will make the case. Instead I am going to share my top five sleep strategies. When executed faithfully, they help significantly.

Waking Routine: Same time. Same habits.

Bedtime Routine: Same time. Same habits. No screens or electronics for at least 30 minutes prior to bed. Take some time to read or reflect on your day. Keep a thankfulness Journal or Daily Examen.

Elevate the Head of Your Bed: This helps with acid reflux. Which helps breathing.

Exercise-Earlier, the Better: Because you energize your body when you exercise, the later in the day your workout, the more difficult it may be to fall asleep.

Maintain Your Sleep Environment: Clutter hurts sleep. Temperature also matters. Keep the room you sleep in on the cool side.

Plan Your Tomorrow, Tonight.

Purge Your Brain: Commit to writing (the old fashioned way or digitally) the thoughts that are racing through your brain. Get 'em out of your head before you lay it down on your pillow.

In our culture, we worship work. The way we relegate everything else – even sleep – to a secondary consideration is dangerous. We try to squeeze sleep into our work-based schedules and if it doesn't fit, we eliminate it altogether. I bet you may even be wondering why this topic is included in this book. Perhaps you were tempted to skip it. *Who has time for sleep when pursuing a dream? There's so much to do.*

The importance of sleep to the human brain is well-documented. Healing, cellular health, mental wellness, creativity are all impacted by sleep. *Don't sleep on sleep!*[45]

Consider this.

"The human brain is the most powerful structure on the planet. It has enabled us to build our bodies and to build skyscrapers-to build automobiles and to build spaceships-to unlock the power of technology to create the Internet and to unlock the power of our DNA to understand life. Our brains can think externally of any circumstance, analyze the past, forecast the future, and create limitless strategies to get there. Billions of brain cells are controlling

45 Shawn Stevenson, *Sleep Smarter: 21 Essential Strategies to Sleep Your Way to a Better Body, Better Health and Bigger Success,* (New York: Rodale, 2016), 6.

every function in your body as well. It's important to understand that each brain cell is capable of doing what your whole body does. These cells eat, communicate, reproduce, and even make waste. Scientists have discovered that this process of waste removal might be one of the biggest connections to our critical need for high-quality sleep."[46]

As you work, create, imagine, plan, and strategize in pursuit of your dream your brain needs time to rest. The brain also needs to clear itself of clutter daily. So, allow it to declutter. Each and every day.

Getting enough sound sleep is one of the biggest challenges for dreamers. We have difficulty turning our brains off. It is hard to stop thinking, analyzing, evaluating. We are processing information constantly. Running through the maze of what's next. Sleep gives us the space to turn it off and recharge. Find a way to help give your brain what it needs to recalibrate for another day of pursuit.

Instead of regarding sleep as an interruption to your pursuit, see it as a necessity. Your dream will thank you!

46 *ibid.*

TRY THIS

How is your sleep?

What do you need to change to put a routine in place so that your sleep can improve?

If you suspect that you have sleep apnea, do yourself and your loved ones a favor and make an appointment for the sleep test today.

Busyness as an Indicator of Productivity Is a Myth

Busyness is not always a badge of honor. It may seem counter-intuitive, but busyness is often evidence of a discipline deficit.

"The busier you are, the more intentional you must be."[47]

Once busyness is planted in our soul, it will grow and choke out any space to realize our dream. Busyness is the enemy. It is a fiend, not a friend. At this point it is helpful to understand the three major reasons WHY busyness takes root in our lives.

Distorted Identity

In our *more evolved,* modern-day human community, the day begins in the morning. This might seem like an obvious statement. That's the point. In some cultures the day begins with relationships, in community. Ours begin with work. Is it any wonder that we place an inordinate amount of emphasis on what we **DO** versus who we **ARE**? This is a harmful distortion.

---

47 Michael Hyatt, *Living Forward: A Proven Plan to Stop Drifting and Get the Life You Want,* (Grand Rapids: Baker Books, 2016).

More and more business executives and CEOs are recognizing this reality and asking for help to change this pattern. Check out this quote from Ron Corucci in Forbes. The title says it all: *Overcome Compulsive Busyness And Find Joy In Being Focused.*

"We live in a world that celebrates and rewards busyness in ways that are addictive. We bounce between exhaustion and boredom, needing the next surge of activity to make us feel important , only to burn out, get bored and repeat the cycle."[48]

Unsettled Purpose

The danger of busyness is that it leads us to believe that mere activity is our purpose, busyness for sake of being busy. So instead of focusing our work, we simply work. It leaves one feeling powerless and unproductive. Over time this leads to an erosion of self-worth. It propels us to say yes to too many good things at the expense of great things. It compromises our ability to prioritize.

Inconsistent Walk with Jesus

The identity-shaping, purpose-defining leadership of Jesus should be an integral part of our life patterns. So often that connection with our Creator becomes secondary. Because of this we are driven, not led. And YOU were designed by God to be led, not driven! It makes sense that the God who created our lives, would have something to say about how we live them. Yet, how often do we seek His advice

---

48 Ron Carucci, *Overcome Compulsive Busyness And Find Joy In Being Focused,* (Forbes, March 15, 2016), https://www.forbes.com/sites/roncarucci/2016/03/15/overcome-compulsive-busyness-and-find-joy-in-being-focused/#239ea8681008.

for how we live our lives? Without God leading the way, we become disoriented, distracted, and more susceptible to busyness.

What misconceptions related to busyness have you embraced?

Tactics to Conquer Busyness

- Schedule your day in advance
- Set aside a busyness-free block of time on a regular basis (daily, weekly, monthly) to breathe, refresh, do something that will energize you and refocus you. Call it self-care or a busyness cleanse. Just do it. Consider it a necessity and commit to it accordingly. Turn back to Lesson 20 and ensure that this busyness-free block of time is in your life rhythm.
- Begin your day with what's most important. Hint: It isn't checking your email or reading texts or social media

    1. Avoid distractions by using the Pomodoro or the Esington Technique. "The Esington Glass is a timeboxing tool designed to boost productivity in a simple, elegant, and beautiful package. The Esington Method uses the Esington Glass 25 minute timer and three simple steps.

    2. Turn off all distractions

    3. Turn over the glass to activate the 3 cues

    4. Work on a single task until your time runs out"[49]

49 *Esington*, https://esington.com/pages/esington-method-explained.

- Stop complaining about how busy you are. Such complaining may come across as bragging, which is ultimately unflattering. What it essentially communicates is that you don't manage your time well.

"This is why I remind you to fan into flames the spiritual gift God gave you... For God has not given us a spirit of fear and timidity, but of power, love, and self-discipline." (New Living Translation, 2 Timothy 1:6-7)

In order to overcome the strong pull toward busyness, it will require power, love, and self-discipline. These three gifts have already been given to you. Receive them. Employ them in your realization.

Before we move on, how about repeating after me? "Busyness is not cool." The next time you feel compelled to tell someone how busy you are, let these four words wash over you. Let's start a movement to put an end to busyness!

TRY THIS

Which myths about busyness have you subscribed to?

Which one of these do I struggle with most?

- **Distorted Identity**
- **Unsettled Purpose**
- **Inconsistent Walk with Jesus**

What am I willing to do to create more unharried space in my life?

If you began your day with what is most important, what would that look like for you?

LESSON 11

Leadership Is Lonely,
yet I Am Never Alone

What is it that creates loneliness? Is it not feeling abandoned?

You are never alone. Listen. "I am with you always."
— Jesus (Matthew 28:20)

When I complain about the loneliness of leadership, I am forgetting this promise.

He will neither leave me nor forsake me.

Here is my discovery, my massive *aha*: I rely too much on the companionship, support, encouragement, and partnership of people. I am a team-player, but I can rely too much on others. Indications of this over-reliance abound. Disappointment. Discouragement. And, of course, loneliness. Waiting for feedback when I post something on Facebook. Compulsively checking email or texts for responses that I deem urgent. Asking teammates to read something before I publish it. Seeking the approval of others for my thoughts and ideas and feeling paralyzed with indecision until I get them. Requiring affirmation for my dreams before I summon the courage to realize them. Desiring the blessings of others along every step in the realization process.

Does any of this sound like problems you encounter in your leadership?

Jesus is the cure for loneliness, self-doubt, and indecision. In short, He's the best remedy for fear.

"I have been crucified with Christ. It is no longer I who live, but Christ who lives in me. And the life I now live in the flesh I live by faith in the Son of God, who loved me and gave himself for me." (English Standard Version, Galatians 2:20)

Jesus is not some cosmic vending machine. He is not a trinket on the shelf that I dust off when I need some magical intervention. He is not an idol I pray to when I'm in a pinch.

He is the LORD of Heaven and Earth AND He has made His life my life. My life, His life.

Do you see? If we are connected to Him, we live with Him. And, He lives with us. He lives not only with you, but IN you. Every experience, good or bad, productive or barren, happy or sad, working or resting is your experience TOGETHER IN JESUS!

You are not alone. Ever.

Living by this truth is so freeing and empowering! In your leadership, in the pursuit of your dream, in your life:

1) Make sure you are not relying too much on others to get you through. Jesus, Jesus, Jesus is your perfect companion on the journey. Companions share the journey, right? So, talk with Him in prayer about what you are experiencing in the pursuit of the dream. Rely on His counsel as He speaks to you through His Word, the Bible. Write down your thoughts as you interact with Him. Through regular and intentional time together you will benefit from His company. Then the other relationships God provides will be a rich blessing.

2) Keep provision and vision straight. Don't mingle them. Like Law & Gospel…distinct, they each have their own gifts to offer. Provision is any person, place, or thing that God gives to you. Those are gifts from Him. He provides them to bless you on the journey. Just as you are for them on theirs. Vision is the clear picture of an inspiring future in which God is pleased and glorified. It leaves you breathless and motivates you to keep going. You can see it. You can taste it. Provision is not vision.

The need for approval is one of my primary challenges. Insecurity consistently pulls me off course and takes my attention off the One who gives me strength to keep pursuing the dream.

Approval…I already have it. I need not waver between the opinions of men.

Please allow me to make myself clear. We never pursue our dreams alone. Relationships and support from others are of tremendous importance in the realization of our dreams. Yet the point I am making in this lesson is to keep relationships in their proper perspective and to make sure that they are helping, not hindering, your dream-realization.

If your dream has been sent by God, there will be those in your circle of relationships that will not approve or support you. Will you stay the course and press on? Or will you shrink back? There will be those who initially resist your dream, but will return later only after they have witnessed its fulfillment.

So, it is critically important that as you realize your dream you pay particular attention to the spiritual disciplines that keep you connected to the source of that dream. The true beauty of a dream is that the pursuit of it strengthens our relationship with Jesus. Kind of like going on a road trip with a loved one you haven't seen in a while; the destination is secondary. At times, however, we focus so much on the business of realizing the dream that we leave our companion behind. In the midst of pursuing the dream we neglect the fact that it is a journey with Jesus. More than ever, these are the times when you will need that connection with Him.

Rededicate yourself. Re-establish those daily rhythms of grace. Resolve to let nothing supplant them. Make them part of your core habits as you pursue your dream.

TRY THIS

Take time to consider how you are leaning on others instead of leaning on Jesus.

How is your day-to-day relationship with Jesus going?

What would change for you if you didn't compartmentalize your faith life?

Do you let Jesus have access into every area of your life? Have you shared your dream with Him?

Take one of these passages per week over the next four weeks and spend enough time with each one that you memorize them.

"For you died, and your life is now hidden with Christ in God" (English Standard Version, Colossians 3:3).

"See what kind of love the Father has given to us, that we should be called children of God; and so we are. The reason why the world does not know us is that it did not know him" (1 John 3:1).

"So we have come to know and to believe the love that God has for us. God is love, and whoever abides in love abides in God, and God abides in him" (1 John 4:16).

"I have been crucified with Christ. It is no longer I who live, but Christ who lives in me. And the life I now live in the flesh I live by faith in the Son of God, who loved me and gave himself for me" (Galatians 2:20).

LESSON 12

Unsettled Leaders Are
Unsettled for Many Reasons

During my sabbatical, I took some time once again to define my life's purpose. Here's the most recent iteration of my mission. *I spark unsettled leaders to dream without fear and freely pursue their NEXT.* In my work with leaders, in and out of the church, around the country, I have noticed increasing unsettledness. I don't think this is necessarily all negative. But it is distracting. Without intervention, it is, at best, debilitating, at worst, destructive.

Unsettledness affects our ability to spark dreams. Being unsettled can also take a toll on dream realization. Pursuing our dream is hard enough on its own. We make it almost impossible when we…

…don't have clarity on our personal calling.

If we aren't clear about who we are and what God is leading us to do next, it is utterly impossible to get there. Our identity and our focus are left up for grabs. If you do not know who you are and why you are, someone will tell you. This is your life, not theirs. God has shaped you. God has called you, set you apart, for His work. And that work is not the same as everyone else's. It is unique. If you don't play your part, who will?

...allow others to drive our decisions and daily workflow.

As ministry leaders, we hear that we are to be available to everyone at anytime. True love, true compassion mandates that we let others define our days and hours. This is not true! Watch Jesus in the Gospels as He shows His apprentices how to love. While He creates spaces for the organic moment to spring up, there is great intentionality to His movement and His mission. Without clear focus leaders can fall victim to the demands of others. They become reactive instead of proactive.

Consider John 11. The events leading up to Lazarus' death are perplexing for some. Why would Jesus wait three days before He gets up and leaves? Why didn't He run to Lazarus as soon as He heard that he was seriously ill?

He gives us an indication in verses 4, 14, and 15

Jesus is clear. His identity and purpose are stunningly clear. He is resolute. Even in an emergency. He does not allow others to dictate His movement. He doesn't ignore Mary and Martha. He is able to place Lazarus' predicament in the context of His mission.

...fall into unproductive work patterns.

The realization of a dream demands focus. Too many times we are diluted or distracted. We are working on too many things at once. Or we are jumping all over the place, flinching with each movement we pick up on in the periphery.

Multitasking is a myth. One thing at a time. Todd Herman uses the term context switching. He describes the real cost of switching from one project to another.[50] Ultimately, it could cost us our dream.

Unsettledness is not in and of itself a bad thing. How we respond to our unsettledness is really the issue. It is imperative that we move forward and free ourselves from ruts. Keeping us in a state of unsettledness is one of the enemy's strategies to deny us our dream.

TRY THIS

Take a moment to consider the three reasons for our unsettledness. Which one particularly plagues you?

I cannot clearly articulate my unique calling.

I allow others to drive my decisions and daily workflow.

I haven't broken free of some unproductive work patterns.

Can you identify any strategies that could free you? How about experimenting with them? What is one thing you could do differently today that might help you tomorrow?

50 Tim Francis, *The Real Cost of Context Switching,* (Forbes, June 12, 2017), https://www. forbes.com/sites/timfrancis/2017/06/12/the-real-cost-of-context-switching/#49ec214f2623

LESSON 13

Stop Worrying About Outcomes

When we go about realizing our dreams, evaluating the choices in front of us by considering their outcomes is a dead end. Determining our actions by how they will turn out is wasted energy. There has to be a better way.

Certainly, shift away from this natural calculus is a challenge. But the stakes are high: doing so is necessary for our inner peace.

Have you ever had difficulty making a decision? Big or small, doesn't matter. You find yourself stuck. Frozen with uncertainty. Well, it's understandable. There are no guarantees. We are not promised how any choice we make will turn out in the end.

We are free to choose. But when we dwell on the outcomes of our potential choices, we become uneasy.

Which way should I go? How should I act? What should I do? Will it work?

Perhaps, your anxiety is out of proportion with how much it really matters. Often two options will ultimately lead to the same destination.

I think of the times when I get so worked up about the route my wife Amy chooses to drive to an event. We're running late. I feel the pressure. She chooses a way I wouldn't. It's longer. At least, to my mind, it's longer. I would have gone the other way. Pressure builds. Anxiety stirs. Guess what? We arrive, no one seems to notice we're a couple minutes late, and we enjoy our evening. Then, we return home, taking MY route.

When I think about all of the energy expended around moments like these... Wow. Anxiety, worry, obsession, losing my composure, and all because of choices and outcomes. None of the worry helped us arrive any quicker; it only made the drive a drag for both of us. I could have shown up in a much better emotional state. I should have let go of the outcome in my mind. Both routes got us there. It made absolutely NO DIFFERENCE which way we chose.

Sometimes the inability to decide and move forward is not because we don't know what to do. We do know what we *want* to do. **We are hesitant, though, because we're obsessing about the outcome.** We want insurance. We want to know how everything will turn out. Keep in mind, that's what we *want*. Here's the truth: there is no way for any one of us to know with absolute certainty how a decision will turn out.

As you pursue the realization of your big dream, you will be confronted with many choices. Please don't stall out trying to predict how your decisions will turn out. Keep moving. There are many ways to get where you want to go. Examine and then execute.

I would like to encourage you today to *examine* and *execute* to your advantage. Since there are no guarantees, and since you are free to decide, DECIDE. You have nothing to lose. Look at decision-making as a grand experiment. Lean toward taking action. Don't fear failure.

There is only one thing. Own your choice. Live with the consequences. Make the commitment. However it turns out, the only thing you need to concern yourself with is responsibility for your choice. After all, you will be responsible whether you like it or not. So, why not charge ahead? Go for it. Stop sweating. Enjoy the ride.

You can be decisive. Not only because there are many roads to the same destination, but because few of your decisions are so irrevocable that you can't go back and try something else if you fail the first time.

TRY THIS

Make a decisive move today giving no thought to how it will turn out. Turn off your "outcome sensor" once today.

How did that feel? What happened?

There Will Always Be Distractions

When it comes to distractions, it is not a matter of *if* you will battle them, but *when*. Utilize all possible resources to equip yourself for this battle. Be prepared. Build your habits now. Your dream depends on it.

There is a cosmic reality at play here. Overcoming distractions is not merely about increased productivity or reaching your long-awaited dream. It is much deeper than that.

The enemy of your soul is real. He is also the enemy of your dream. Especially when that dream is God-given. You can call him Satan, the devil, or the Evil One. He is not only the father of lies. He is also the prince of distractions. He is the king of waste. He is determined to keep you from being of service, a, blessing, to the world. He will have you do anything but pursue your dream.

My mind has been trained over time to give in to distraction.

Soundbites, text messages, and rapid-fire images have contracted our attention spans over time. It will take some practice and training to stretch them out again so that we can focus for longer stretches of time on a single topic.

There is science behind distractions and how our brains work. Check out this blog post from Nautilus:

"In terms of changing our brains, laboratories and companies around the world are now engaged in large-scale development and research efforts directed at understanding how we can enhance our brain's functioning to improve cognitive control and thus reduce the negative impact of goal interference. Approaches include traditional education, meditation, cognitive training, video games, exposure to nature, drugs, physical exercise, neuro-feedback, and brain stimulation. Interestingly, many of them use modern technology to harness neuroplasticity and induce brain changes. We are at the threshold of fascinating times, as the technology that has aggravated the Distracted Mind is now being formulated to offer remediation."[51]

It is easier to give in to distraction than it is to stay focused.

Shallow, surface thinking is much easier to do than deep contemplation and introspection. We avoid the latter, it appears, because we may find out something that we do not want to know about ourselves, something that needs to change. Perhaps the command to "fear not" is more applicable here than anywhere else. Being alone with our thoughts can be intimidating.

"We are self-interrupting and not even aware of how often we are diverting our attention from our main task."[52]

---

51 Adam Gazzaley and Larry D. Rosen, *Are You a Self-Interrupter?*, (Nautilus, May 25, 2017),
    http://m.nautil.us/issue/48/chaos/are-you-a-self_interrupter.
52 *ibid.*

We find it unsettling to be alone with our thoughts.[53] For this reason, the rhythms I shared in Lesson 10 require us to be still and listen, to be alone with the Author and Shaper of our Dreams.

In pursuing your dream, what you are working on has cosmic significance.

The deeper the significance and Kingdom-of-God impact of your dream, the more relentless the distractions.

We live in a distraction-rich environment by design.

"People respond like Pavlov's dogs to incoming email communication, waiting only an average of one minute and 44 seconds to open that message."[54]

"Our technology continues to find new ways to attract our attention because this is what brings "eyeballs," and the common marketing wisdom is that eyeballs bring money."[55]

As if the notifications on our smartphones were not enough to distract us, now there are LED table lamps that light up any time you get a notification. Yikes! The product is actually called Notti. https://www.wittidesign.com/products/notti

Naughty, indeed.

Pursuing your dream in today's distraction-rich environment will demand focus. In order to achieve that focus we will have to establish

53 *ibid.*
54 *ibid.*
55 *ibid.*

some new pathways in our brains. It will be a challenge, but with wisdom, confidence, and commitment to a God-given dream, success is within your grasp.

TRY THIS

Here are some ideas to put into practice.

1.   Don't check email, texts, or Social Media first thing in the morning.

2.   Place your phone and iPad in another room while you are attempting to stay focused.

3.   Disengage your alerts and notifications on whatever device you are working on.

4.   Plan your day the night before. There's a better chance of staying the course if you have mapped out your course for the day.

5.   Block out space in your day for correspondence through email, texting, and social media. Do not give in. Resist the urge. For example: reserve 11-11:30 am and 4:30-5 pm for emails and texts and social media.

Add your own to the list. Drop me a note at jeff@jeffmeyer.org and share your ideas with me.

Pick one and implement it today. Experiment with it.

Stuck? Change It Up

You are free. Exercise that freedom. Give yourself permission. You've heard it said, "You are perfectly designed to get the results you are currently getting." It's really simple: if you don't like the dance, change the music. If you feel stuck, try something different.

Shift your morning routine. Change the exercise program. Adapt the training regimen. Try a new shampoo. Rearrange your office space. Use a different day planner. Go to a different coffee shop. Experiment with a different way of reading scripture. Utilize technology in a different way. Ask someone to help you stay accountable to the new rhythm. Do something different to prepare for worship.

I talked with a friend recently who said he has dreaded going to worship for the past two years. He has young, active children. It's hard for him to get anything out of worship when he is wrangling with his little ones. The dance isn't working for him. He loves his children. They are eager to go to church. He isn't. It's hard work. So, we prayed together that God would show him a creative solution that would re-engage his heart in worship. I'd like to tell you that his worship experience with his children in tow is nirvana now. It's still a struggle. But he is entering with different expectations. Instead of expecting his kids to behave a certain way, he now looks at their eagerness and attempts to affirm that eagerness by engaging them even more deeply in what they are experiencing.

Don't resign yourself to being stuck. Creative solutions abound. Why not try asking Him for one? Sit and listen to Him.

There are reasons why you are stuck.

Copycatting

Maybe you are attempting to do something someone told you to do, conforming to others' expectations. Perhaps you are trying to live off of someone else's successful rhythm. And it isn't working for you any longer. Or maybe it never worked for you. Stop it.

Stop copying someone else just because they told you what works for them. Find your own way. Experiment. If that doesn't work, try something else.

What Once Worked Is Not Working Anymore

Simple, right? Something that worked for you for years is no longer motivating for you. Ok. Welcome to life. You've grown. You're a different person than you were ten years ago, five years ago, even one year ago. You've learned things.

You've discovered things about yourself. You are simply in a different stage of life. You never used to have children. Now you do. You raised your kids. Now they are out of the house. Your little children are now self-sufficient. You're older and your body isn't quite as resilient as it once was. Embrace the change and find a new way.

God Desires to Do Something New in Your Life

Have you ever considered that maybe your "stuckness" is prompted by God because He wants to show you something new? Perhaps He wants you to discover something deeper, more vibrant. You have been drinking milk. It's time to eat meat (1 Corinthians 3:2). Our God is a God of new things. He is always doing something new (Isaiah 43:19). You can't put new wine in old wineskins (Mark 2:22). Sometimes the container needs to be replaced. If you have some suspicion that this might be one of the reasons why you are stuck, you can ask another person how they do what you want to do. Better yet, ask God to reveal some new container for you. Then quiet your planning mind and listen long enough for Him to show you some options. Finally, pick one and give it a try.

One final word of encouragement: embrace the freedom that you have been given. We may feel stuck in each our own way, but trust that there are countless creative solutions to this general problem. So, you are free to experiment. Look at every attempt as an experiment in a grand adventure.

Are you burdening yourself with heavy expectations? Ok. Take a deep breath and consider this lesson your permission slip, your hall pass, to get out. Try something new.

TRY THIS

Where are you feeling stuck? What used to work for you that is no longer working?

What are you willing to try that would change your routine?

Remember: there is no failure in the experiments you try, just more information learned.

When You Want to Change, Strategies Are More Helpful Than Willpower

The spirit is willing, but the flesh is weak. Jesus spoke these words. They couldn't be any truer. We set our mind on the change that we seek. And still, it doesn't work. We run into barriers. We fail to execute. Sometimes we don't really want to change so when we hit one of those walls, we use it as an excuse to quit.

We may think that some people have what it takes to push through the barriers and others don't. Why try if you don't have the willpower? The need to change is recognized, but the change is never realized because we have already predetermined that we are not capable. We are just weak, inadequate, helpless. We are not equal to the task in front of us.

A better routine will help. Human willpower needs some help. Alone, willpower fails.

Distractions. Discouragement. Laziness. These three prey on the vulnerable human will. Willpower is a perishable resource. Rely on it alone at your own peril.

So if someone knows they need to make behavior change, what is he or she supposed to do?

Establish some positive, momentum-building routines for yourself. I call them strategies. They get you moving in the right direction. I tend to wait for inspiration to strike before I move. A little structure and a few strategies go a long way in freeing up my creativity and helping me overcome inertia. These strategies minimize the waiting-for-inspiration time.

Here are a few examples.

- Meditate for 10 minutes first thing in the morning
- Memorize Scripture
- Call a friend
- Stop and breathe
- Get up and take a quick walk before getting back to work
- Use the Pomodoro technique *(a time management system that breaks down work into 20 or 25 minute segments interrupted by a short break)*
- Write down all the thoughts in your head before putting your head on your pillow
- Brush your teeth first thing in the morning
- Reward yourself with that caffeinated beverage you love only AFTER you have accomplished your morning routine
- Praise God for ONE thing every day
- Create a God Box and put in it the things that are overwhelming you
- Put your cell phone in another room when you sleep or when you work

- Enlist a trusted friend to help you be [more] accountable
- Don't read email until you have executed your morning routine

Develop your own go-to strategies.

You'll notice that there are physical strategies and emotional strategies. The key is to experiment and see what works for you. Where do your interests lie? What do you enjoy? Do that. What seems like a chore? Don't do that. Over time you will begin to understand what works for you and what doesn't. Pretty simple. Scrap what doesn't. Employ what does.

In the post, "What Mentally Strong People Do On Tough Days,"[56] from her website, Positive Prescription, Dr. Samantha Boardman, a psychiatrist, writes:

> "We all have emergency plans. If the electricity goes out, there's a stockpile of flashlights, batteries, and candles. But what happens when your mood fails? What's your bad day backup plan? It's a question I ask people all the time."

Michele Phillips, a performance coach and author of *Happiness Is a Habit*, has a group of friends who have dubbed themselves the Village.

> "I can call them anytime my day is going badly, and they will change my frame of mind," she says. She

---

56 Samantha Boardman, What Mentally Strong People Do On Tough Days, (Positive Prescription), https://positiveprescription.com/mentally-strong-people-tough-days/.

recalls sitting in a bar in Colorado after her divorce, feeling lonely and, she says, "like I had 'loser' written on my forehead. I called a Village friend, and she said, 'Look around: You're in Vail, skiing!' She helped me shift the thinking from 'poor me' to 'lucky me.'"

In your pursuit of the dream, there will be times when you will get stuck. Not *if,* mind you, but *when.* So, do yourself a huge favor and establish some strategies for those moments. I find that when my emotions get the best of me or when I have been stationary too long and the sloth monster threatens to overtake me, two things help me keep going. Movement and breathing. Here are a few strategies I employ: get up and move, do work on my walking desk, do ten push-ups or jumping jacks, sit on the floor, close my eyes and breathe deep breaths. I have also found that these are the moments when I need to drink more water.

In order to activate your dream you will need to overcome inertia. You will have bad days, slow days. Implement your strategies, devise and follow through with go-to moves that rebuild momentum, and execute your plan.

TRY THIS

Are there any of the strategies listed that you find interesting and would consider implementing?

What is your "bad day back up plan"?

Who can you call when you need to reframe? Who is in your "Village"?

In Addressing Bad Habits, Think "Replace," Not "Remove"

As you get serious about pursuing a dream, you will notice that certain long-standing habits will constitute obstacles. Over time those habits may have created unhealthy patterns and dependencies. If progress is to be gained, if positive change is to be effected, one must deal with such habits.

When we become aware of these bad habits our first reaction is to try to eliminate them. It doesn't work. Tell me to stop doing something, and I will probably want to do it even more.

The only way to change unhealthy habits is to replace them with healthy habits.

Your day consists of a series of habits. Your life, the sum total of all the habits you developed and sustained over the years. Habits aren't all bad. In fact, they are necessary. They help us live. We rely on habits so that we do not become overwhelmed by the complexity of life. Habits allow us a break from making decisions. Understanding how habit loops work is an important piece to understanding how to change our habits from those that work against us to those that work for us.

Each of your habits, bad and good, has a *habit loop*. In Chapter 1 of *The Power of Habit: Why We Do What We Do in Life and Business*,[57] best selling author and New York Times reporter, Charles Duhigg describes a habit loop as a three-step rhythm: "cue, routine, reward."

He explains, "When a habit emerges, the brain stops fully participating in decision making. So unless you deliberately fight a habit—unless you find new routines—the pattern will unfold automatically."

Duhigg argues that our best chance of effecting change is to discover the loop and then determine where in that loop the unwanted habit is located. "By the same rule, though, if we learn to create new neurological routines that overpower those behaviors—if we take control of the habit loop—we can force those bad tendencies into the background."

In Chapter 3 Duhigg explains the Golden Rule of Habit Change. "...to change a habit, you must keep the old cue, and deliver the old reward, but insert a new routine. That's the rule: If you use the same cue, and provide the same reward, you can shift the routine and change the habit. Almost any behavior can be transformed if the cue and reward stay the same."

Replace, not *remove*. Replace the routine that is stimulated by the same cue. Replace the routine that results in the same reward. Find an alternative routine, believe that it is possible to change, and include others in your journey.

---

57 Charles Duhigg, The *Power of Habit: Why We Do What We Do in Life and Business*, (New York: Random House, 2012).

Here are some habit loop examples that you may want to change because they are unproductive or unhealthy:

Cue: boredom in the middle of the day
Routine: surfing the web
Reward: stimulation

Cue: driving in your car
Routine: light up a cigarette
Reward: adrenaline rush

Cue: getting home after work
Routine: turning on TV
Reward: decompress and chill

Cue: stuck with writer's block in the middle of writing
Routine: checking email
Reward: a sense of connection

Ask yourself:

What are my cues? What is the feeling or situation that immediately precedes the routine?

Then brainstorm alternatives:

What other activities could I do instead of the unproductive routine I am currently seeking to eliminate? *Instead of surfing the web, for example, I could have a notepad next to me, and I could simply doodle on it for stimulation while gathering my thoughts. Instead of sitting*

down and turning on the TV when I get home from work, I could open
a book and read for a few minutes until I feel composed.

Identifying the habit loop and replacing the routine will go a long
way in helping us replace the habits that are getting in the way of our
productivity and dream realization.

TRY THIS

In regard to your dream pursuit, make a list of
the habits you want to replace.

Pick one. Instead of just trying to eliminate it, take the time to
discover where on the loop the bad habit falls and replace it.

Cue – Routine – Reward

Keep the cue and reward the same, but change the routine.

Ready? Go for it!

Behavioral Change Requires PRACTICE (Repetition over Time)

In pursuit of your dream you will ultimately stumble across something in your behavior that needs to be changed.

Instituting any change in behavior takes practice and patience.

There is a false assumption about behavioral change in the church. I suppose this is true outside of the church as well. Many believe that they have learned something if they have heard it. They believe that believing in something is adequate.

There is a difference between believing in and believing. There is a distinction between trusting in and trusting. Jesus invites us to the latter. He is not interested in merely having His followers believe *in* Him. He invites us to put that trust into action. And that takes practice.

Jesus came to earth to save us. He also came to transform us. Salvation and transformation are intertwined. So, along the way, there will be times when His Word, His call, will prompt us to change something. We cannot simply intellectualize the change. We need to actualize it.

There is a process to behavioral change that is helpful for us to understand. The awareness of this journey toward change will grant us familiarity in uncharted waters. After all, any behavior we are motivated to change will take us into the unknown. In these instances it is always good to have some solid footing.

Read through these five Stages of Behavioral Change and consider where you are and what your greatest need is right now. There is certainly some behavioral change you are being prompted to make as you realize your dream.

Becoming Aware

At some level, any behavioral change begins here. Some external influence will stimulate a thought that you really never considered before. In reading a blog post on productivity hacks you discover a new way to begin your morning. In your inbox you get a marketing piece on the right stretch to do first thing in the morning. A friend shares an idea about how to read the Bible. A word or phrase from your daily Bible reading grabs your attention and sparks an idea you've never thought of before.

Greatest need during this stage: Be open and thoughtful as you go.

Consideration

At this point you begin to process what it might look like if you made the change. What would be different? How hard would it be?

How do you do it? Who could help you? Are you really interested in making the change? Is it worth it?

This is also the time when barriers and obstacles will come into play. Especially if this change is prompted by God. This is when second thoughts chime in. You might even talk yourself out of it, coming up with all kinds of excuses and citing all kinds of obstacles that will "make it impossible to execute." Many invitations to behavioral change die here.

Greatest need during this stage: Asking powerful questions.

Decision

In order to make progress, we must bring to a close the consideration stage and make a decision. We have come through the tunnel of assessing our options. We have done the research. We have planned. We have asked for help. We have read up. We are now determined to make a go of it. We need to tell someone so that we are accountable. And then we must quietly resolve to move forward.

Greatest need during this stage: Declare your intention. Make a commitment. Write it down. Schedule it. Share with a friend. Make it public.

Execution

We begin to implement our plan. We act. It is very important in this stage to be kind to ourselves. It might be helpful to realize that effective execution begins with practice. Give yourself space to try different things. There are a variety of approaches to making the change you want to make. Creativity isn't just allowed; it's required. One of the things that occasionally trips me up is that when I get an idea, I tend to try and **adopt** the change as is, in its entirety. I forget that I need to **adapt** it. I can tweak an idea to fit my context, personality, and needs. I don't have to simply activate the change exactly the way I read about it in the blog post. Here's an example. I wanted to eat healthier. So, Amy and I found a popular diet system online. We tried it for a week. Following every step and recommendation, we quickly became overwhelmed. This system was too much for us. We quit. What might have happened if we would have adapted the system? I can think for myself. I have the freedom to experiment in my execution. This takes practice.

Greatest need during this stage: Practice. Act. Do. Evaluate how it is working for you. Adapt. Rinse and repeat.

Persevere

If these important changes are to take root, it will take a certain amount of courage from you to maintain the behavior. The change will need to be lived out for a period of time before it becomes second nature. Not every change you decide to incorporate will stick. This is the time to evaluate whether the change was vital for the long haul or perhaps only needed for a season.

Greatest need during this stage: Establish a support network.

TRY THIS

Is there a behavioral change that you have recently been prompted to make?

Where are you in these stages?

What is your greatest need right now?

What are you going to do about it?

I Don't Need a New Assignment

I need to live faithfully in the positions, or posts, I already have been given.

As an entrepreneur with an apostolic calling I find myself drawn to starting new things. I enjoy trying and learning new things. I like the freshness that new things offer, the lack of clutter, the richness of possibility.

I am also a Type Four on the Enneagram, someone who is excited. In this you have a wonderfully dangerous combination. Type Fours have the tendency to think that the sky is falling. Difficulties that emerge in life are rich soil for Type Fours to grow. Difficulties happen in any and every new endeavor. And Type Fours tend to place the blame for every difficulty on themselves. (For more information for Type Fours on the Enneagram, see *Appendix*.)

I have learned that I tend to think that if I were in a different spot, things would automatically be better. Have you ever given in to the "grass is greener" concept in your own situation?

In 2017 *the Church at Christ Memorial* gave my wife Amy and me a very precious opportunity. We took a six-month sabbatical, which gave me an opportunity to leave without leaving, so to speak. I continue to be grateful for the chance we were given to "experiment" and to seek God's wisdom. It was an unsettling time. After 19 years at *the Church* I wasn't sure that God wanted me to continue. Was He calling me to other ventures?

What I learned during those six months was that He had not called me away from the local church. He actually renewed a vision for my work in Madison. He had not lifted His hand of blessing either. Even when things looked like they were not going according to my plan or my expectations, He was still working. My leadership, my skills, my insight were still needed. It appeared that I was still appreciated.

It is true that God does His work and carries out His will often without us being conscious of it. That said, plenty of times He chooses to include us and use us. He is the Master Creator. He has made you. He has gifted you. In your baptism He has called you. Yes, you.

It is quite natural for our minds to wander when difficulties arise and doubts creep in. We wander to what seem to be greener pastures. But all too often what appears to be an oasis turns out to be a mirage.

Sometimes those extended times of difficulties and doubts mean that it is time for a change. Sometimes they are seasons in which God is pruning us for greater fruitfulness. Fruitfulness does not come without challenge. And sometimes fruitfulness will not look anything like what we think it should. God alone determines the outcome.

So, how do we determine if it is time to move on or stay. Should I stay or should I go? Cue The Clash song.

Am I still committed to the vision? Is there still a deep desire and passion to see that dream fulfilled? Is the vision still meaningful and relevant to the context in which I serve? Are my gifts still needed in this calling? If I don't stay and work at it, who will? Will the dream be lost?

Are the challenges that I am facing in this moment a clear sign from God that my time here has come to a close or are they instances of the Holy Spirit pruning so that I, and others, may grow? Are there rough edges in my character that these difficulties and doubts are meant to smooth out? Has God allowed this challenge so that I will become even more useful for Him, even more effective?

These are not easy questions to answer. Quite the opposite. They can bring you to your knees. They can't be answered without a deep dependency on God and others. They take time and space. And that's why the sabbatical was such a blessing.

Sometimes we quit too soon. Yes, even after a very long time, we can quit too soon. A little tip I would give is that if you really are unsure of whether it is time to quit, it is probably time to stick it out. Seth Godin in his wonderful work "Dip: The Little Book that Teaches You When to Quit"[58] lists three questions to ask before you quit.

1. Am I panicking? It's never a good idea to quit when you are panicking.

58 Seth Godin, *Dip: The Little Book that Teaches You When to Quit*, (London: Portfolio, 2007), 66-71.

2. Who am I trying to influence? If there is an itch to leave, it is quite possible that it is directly related "to your current attempt at influence." Make a distinction between influencing one person and a group of people, say, a market. "One person will make up his mind and if you're going to succeed, you'll have to change it. And changing someone's mind is difficult, if not impossible." Pg. 68 "If you're trying to influence a market, though, the rules are different…most of the people in the market have never even heard of you. The market doesn't have just one mind.

    "Influencing one person is like scaling a wall. If you get over the wall the first few tries, you're in. If you don't, often you'll find the wall gets higher with each attempt. Influencing a market, on the other hand, is more of a hill than a wall. You can make progress, one step at a time, and as you get higher, it actually gets easier"

3. What sort of measurable progress am I making?

    Steps need to be taken toward milestones. Any forward movement is good.

    If you are not panicking, if you are working at influencing a market with your dream and are making even small progress toward that dream, it's probably a sign that you should hang in there. If you decide to stick with it, what you will need is some mental fortitude, toughness, willingness to explore new methodologies and angles.

If we're to think of the church as a group- or market-targeted endeavor, then it would appear that today's church is full of people, pastors, and non-clergy who are too quick to flee. I would guess it is true in other group-targeted endeavors as well. Friendships, colleagues at work, business partners and associates, marriages. When things get tough, when the challenge is high and the struggle becomes real, most people check out. They quit. They run. The church is no different than the rest of the world.

One of the unexpected realities in a long-tenured ministry is that you see this over and over again. Commitment, resolve, and stability are wanting. I think it is one of the greatest weaknesses in American Christianity.

One final thought. The search for a new post can either be an escape strategy from a difficult mission or an opportunity for you to shift perspective or approach. Discern the motivation and discover the truth.

TRY THIS

Go back and review Set Godin's three questions and apply it to your current situation. How do you answer them in regard to the realization of your dream? What do you notice?

1. Am I panicking?
2. Who am I trying to influence?
3. What sort of measurable progress am I making?

Here are some additional questions to consider:

- Could the challenges, difficulties, and even discouragement you face as a leader actually be opportunities to work toward stability?
- What's at stake if you don't hang in there?

Is the mission worth it? Is it a lost cause, a waste of time? Or, is the payoff on the other side of the struggle worth the battle?

When You Read, 'Fear Not,' Know That God Is with You

Fear is a brutal taskmaster. It keeps us from being who we were made to be and from doing what we were made to do.

Fear keeps us from saying we're sorry because doing so may hurt our pride. Fear keeps us from investing because we might lose. Fear keeps us from taking a risk because it might not work out. Fear keeps us from speaking up because we might be contradicted, if not ridiculed.

People might get upset. Or be disappointed in us. It could be that taking an action might be misinterpreted and that, as a result, we suffer unfair judgment.

Organizations and institutions are set up based on a motivation of fear. We call them checks and balances. We're afraid someone might have too much power. Israel asked for a king like all the other nations because they were afraid they might stand out or miss out (1 Samuel 8). Look how that turned out.

How many budgets are set up and approved out of fear? How many situations are processed and "solutioneered" based on fear?

Joseph was afraid to take Mary as his wife. Moses was afraid to return to Egypt. The early Christian church was afraid to welcome Gentiles as equals. The Pharisees to listen to Jesus. The disciples to leave the upper room.

On and on the human reality spins. Fear lurks about, influencing, manipulating, controlling.

Fear not.

Don't be afraid.

These entreaties are more than a command to banish fear. They're a promise. They are THE signature message that God is near.

Fear not. **God is near.**

Fear not. For unto you is born this day in the City of David... (English Standard Version, Luke 2:11).

Fear not, for I have redeemed you. I have called you by name, you are mine (Isaiah 43:1).

Do not be afraid---I am with you. I am your God---let nothing terrify you! I will make you strong and help you; I will protect you and save you (Good News Translation, Isaiah 41:10).

"We have nothing to fear but fear itself" – President Roosevelt. We place so much attention on the result, on how what we *might* do *might* turn out. But we are not God. We have no idea how anything will turn out. There are zero guarantees given to us. We will NEVER know what the result of our actions will be. Giving in to our fear in an effort to control the results is utter foolishness, isn't it? We're much better off simply letting go of the results and taking that next step we have been invited to take. Accept your finite nature and trust the infinite ONE who is God.

That's the secret: **replacing fear with faith.** When you recognize fear stirring, quickly turn to trust. Ask yourself, what is God asking me to give to Him right now? What about this situation is God wanting me to hand over to His control? How would God address you right now? In the moment, stop yourself from spiraling, assume God's supreme vantage point, and complete the following statement.

Fear not. I am _____

I was in the middle of a conflict with someone. It was not getting resolved. The distance was increasing. The chasm seemed too much to overcome. God was nudging me to break the silence and say that I was sorry for my part in the tension. I resisted for a long time. I was afraid I would be taken advantage of. I feared that this person would never recognize their own contribution to the problem if I admitted mine. Finally, I relented. And, then after I broke the ice, I was afraid I had made a mistake. Man, am I a creature of fear, or what? I'm not an exception, am I? Aren't we are all creatures of fear, to some extent

Think about a recent instance in which you let fear get the best of you. What were you focused on? In fact, make a list of five different situations where fear reigned. Do you recognize a pattern? Identifying it coolly and calmly in retrospect will benefit you the next time the heat is turned up.

Take some time in the next few days to memorize a few of your favorite promises of God's presence and provision in the Scriptures. Make them personal. Tuck them away in your heart. Write them down. Carry them around so you can pull them out when you need reassurance.

The next time you recognize fear rearing its ugly head, stop yourself. Turn instead to trust. Remember God's promise. Speak aloud one of your go-tos. Remind yourself that you are God's. He is sovereign. He is in control. You cannot control by giving into fear. He's got this. He's got you.

TRY THIS

As you realize your big dream, what are some of your fears? Make a list of five or so.

Then, consider those individual fears and next to them complete the sentence fragment below with a specific promise for each fear. Let God speak these words over you.

Fear not. I am _____

The Plan Forward Begins with One Step, the NEXT One

See if this rings true with you.

The long view is overwhelming. All the changes I need to be make are crushing. All the things I want to do, paralyzing. The dream seems way too big and out of my reach. I'm incapacitated. It is hard to get motivated to do anything meaningful because it all seems so pointless.

Look, the long view is meant to be broad, out of reach, "down the line," so to speak. Its purpose is to help us set the direction, not describe the next step. The point of the Big dream is to motivate, not provide the particulars of tomorrow's agenda.

In order for your big dream to live, it must be broken down and divided into parts. The ultimate out-of-reach destination begins with the NEXT step.

I think that is one of the reasons why God says that...

"We can make our plans, but the LORD determines our steps" (New Living Translation, Proverbs 16:9).

"But the noble make noble plans, and by noble deeds they stand" (New International Version, Isaiah 32:8).

There is this ongoing tension in life between the dream and the execution. We must learn to be flexible and fluid in our execution because God directs our steps.

The freedom in realization comes in taking the NEXT step. We pursue the dream ONLY by taking the NEXT step. Your NEXT is your ticket to progress and ultimately, achievement. Figure that out and you are on your way. Someone very wise once said, "Do something before you do everything." Tomorrow starts today.

Be who you ultimately want to be TODAY. There is magic in TODAY. Think about all the ways God instructs us to TODAY. TODAY, this day.

I'm a TOMORROW person, so for me TODAY is not only foundationally important, but a challenge as well. There is a great clip from the movie, *Smoke*, that I use in my consulting work with Auxano. The shop owner, played by Harvey Keitel, is helping a neighbor, played by William Hurt, take a breather and appreciate the gift of awareness. "Tomorrow, tomorrow, tomorrow...", he says. "Slow down?" "I recommend it." Keitel's character says this as Hurt's character is working his way through Keitel's collection of photographs of the same corner each and every morning. This whole scene illustrates the gift of being aware of the subtle differences that beg for attention today, right now.

At the halfway point of my six-month sabbatical from my local church I almost became obsessed with my re-entry plan. I was losing the benefit of TODAY! A friend reminded me to stop and live in TODAY. I discovered in this experience that it was really a matter of trust. My incessant focus on tomorrow was deep down a lack of confidence in God. I was trying to control the future by dwelling on it. Silly, right? Sure, but part of the human condition, nevertheless. We attempt to control our future and in the least effective way, through anxiety, worry, obsessively considering all the options, and dwelling on what could be or should be. God desires that we live in the HERE and NOW. That's probably why there are so many instructions from God telling us to not worry about tomorrow, to not be anxious about anything, to cast our cares on Him.

We have a relationship with the living God of the universe. One of the names given to the Messiah is *Immanuel*, which means "God with us." It's not "God waiting for us."

God is with me, TODAY. I know that He is also the God who is the same yesterday and forever, too. But, don't forget TODAY.

TRY THIS

What is the NEXT step you need to take?

How can you intentionally Slow Down?

Embrace the Paradox: Everything Is Not on My Shoulders, and, Everything Changes When I Do

Realizing our dreams will require change. Dreams usually emerge in our conscience because we are committed to see something change. Leading change contains a great paradox. Everything is not on my shoulders. And, everything changes when I do.

One of the greatest and most freeing realizations in my leadership life was that the ministry that I have given so much of my love, thought, and effort to, can and will survive without me. If the dream is a spark from the Divine, it will most certainly continue on after I am gone. On the surface, it almost seems like a contradiction coming after Lesson 19. In fact, some did see my sabbatical as quitting. "He just quits when the going gets tough."

It's a paradox. The lessons I have learned during this time have been so big for me. For so much of my leadership life I have felt the weight of responsibility without the freedom of being a teammate with others. Don't misunderstand, I love my teammates. I love their input, their contribution. In fact, I have always gotten more joy out of watching others participate, lead, and succeed. Ultimately, however, I feel that

I carry the burden for ALL of it. I fashion myself as a sojourn leader, working alongside (sojourn) a fellow traveler in my position as a senior leader. It's one of my essential values. An aspirational value, perhaps. Because rarely, when push comes to shove, have I been able to really share the accountability?

The thrill of joining with others in missionary work keeps me in the game. Yet, I must say, that those moments have not been as frequent as I would like. They have not been the norm.

The success of any dream worth pursuing cannot rest solely on the shoulders of the dreamer. Many times the pursuit of the dream is a team effort. And not just a team receiving orders from the boss and following them. For plenty of changes to endure, they must be initiated and implemented by a host of dreamers.

Positions of power and influence come with a temptation. The person in charge may come to believe: *The call to change anything in realizing my dream is on me. The call to pursue a dream is mine alone. And, therefore, it is my responsibility to get everyone else to change in order to achieve that organizational change.*

The kind of lasting change upon which dreams are founded cannot occur under demand or coercion. Change is a shared endeavor.

Still, executive functioning is essential for some things. What can you control? Your own mindset and execution. You cannot control anyone else's. In your confusion over the bounds of your control, the burden grows and becomes overwhelming.

Being clear about your role, gifts, and contributions and making sure others are clear about theirs is the key to a well-functioning team. Self-awareness and invitation, these are the hallmarks of effective leadership.

TRY THIS

If everything changes when we do… what are you willing to change about you?

My Broken Spaces Are Not
to Be Covered Up or Compensated For

In pursuit of your big, divinely sparked dream, you will inevitably stumble. You will fail. You will struggle. You will run into roadblocks. You will hit walls mid-stride. You will discover your own brokenness.

One of the biggest, most important realization strategies is to ACKNOWLEDGE YOUR BROKENNESS, and invite Jesus to shine through the gaps. This is vital. Absolutely critical.

And yet, we…

…avoid vulnerability.

...cover up mistakes.

...compensate for weakness.

So this call to lay bare our brokenness deserves some elaboration.

Relationships Are Everything

Relationships are built on trust, and there is no trust without vulnerability.

Have you ever been in a relationship with someone who never said, "I'm sorry"? Did you trust them? Were you confident at all that you two could weather the storm?

God's Power Is Made Perfect in Your Weakness

But he said to me, "My grace is sufficient for you, for my power is made perfect in weakness." Therefore I will boast all the more gladly about my weaknesses, so that Christ's power may rest on me. That is why, for Christ's sake, I delight in weaknesses, in insults, in hardships, in persecutions, in difficulties. For when I am weak, then I am strong (New International Version, 2 Corinthians 12:9-10).

The most inspirational stories are those of struggle. No one spends time watching a story of someone overcoming nothing. There is little inspiration hearing about someone who has it all and never wants for anything. It's boring to listen to someone tell you about how everything went right for them. Why is that?

The beautiful stories of redemption are the inspiring ones. The miraculous stories of forgiveness are the ones that give me hope. None of those stories are possible unless someone lets down their guard and reveals weakness.

Contained within every overcomer's story is the essence of the Gospel. Dying and rising. Beat down and restored. Conflict and reconciliation.

So then, we should allow people to see our personal weaknesses, our struggles, the brokenness within us. Because behind that and through that is the Light.

The key to pushing through the inevitable mistakes and setbacks that accompany the pursuit of any dream is always returning to this love of God which is eternal, uncommon and, ultimately, undeserved.

At times the pursuit is fueled by impure motivations. Not to worry. **God will redirect it.**

Other times our dreams are too small. Fear not. **God will enlarge it.**

Frequently our execution won't be effective. Have faith. **God will straighten your crooked road.**

This is real love–not that we loved God, but that he loved us and sent His Son as a sacrifice to take away our sins (New Living Translation, 1 John 4:10).

My love is imperfect. It is flawed.

My love is inconsistent. It comes and goes, laced with selfish agenda.

My love is illustrative. It reveals my true nature.

God's love is unblemished. It is pure.

God's love is unchanging. It is the same yesterday, today, and forever.

God's love is unrestrained. It is unbounded in its power and grace.

As long as I return to His love, I'll be OK. If I remain focused on my own, weight and guilt will burden me.

This plan will never disappoint you. It may sound simple. Believe me, it's not. Truth is, we don't always appreciate people intervening when it comes to our dreams. Even God. It is never an easy thing for a dreamer like you to surrender your dream to anyone. We will protect it with a fierceness that sometimes places us in a precarious position. Fearing a battle of wills, you will be tempted to take steps in your execution without first consulting the Dream-maker.

But this temptation can lead to missteps and poor judgment. Our judgment and perspective is not 100% pure all the time. It can be laced with fear, self-preservation, and limited understanding. It is crucial to return to the source regularly. We must return to Him in humility and honesty and with an open heart. Because whether or not we ultimately realize our dreams, they pale in comparison to God's promised love and presence.

God's plan to reconcile the world to Himself does not include any measure of human performance. His plan to love you does not include any measure of the performance of your dream-realization strategies. While He cares about your dream, to be sure, He cares even more about YOU.

Now, don't misunderstand. God does care about missteps and poor judgement. As a holy God, He cannot simply brush our errors and sins under the carpet. But His plan is executed perfectly in the performance and placement of His Son. God is aware of your faults, sins, and imperfections. And no trespass or transgression is too much for the redemption offered in His Son, Jesus!

Because of this, I can move past my imperfections, the inconsistency of my love. Right past my missteps and poor judgment... to His love.

TRY THIS

How aware are you of your broken spaces? Do you find yourself trying to cover up for your mistakes or compensate for weakness?

Where is the light able to shine through the broken spaces in your life? Where is God beginning to redeem those weaknesses for His glory?

Have you made any missteps or shown any poor judgement that you need to confess?

Return to God's love.

Repent, turn away from the misstep, confess that you used poor judgement.

Realign your dream and your plans with the One who gave them to you, and surrender your ways to Him.

Re-engage in the work He lays out in front of you.

Hold your dream before God with open hands. Surrender it to him.

.

Add Value

Mastermind groups are multiplying. These Facebook or similar online groups connect people who are pursuing similar dreams. I have joined some of them for guidance on processes I knew little about. I have joined them to learn how to use equipment or technology. I have joined them for simple encouragement to not give up. Realizing a dream is tough work. It's not for the faint of heart. We need each other. In all of these groups there is a common plea:

> *As you participate in this learning and support community, ...contribute, don't just take.*

> *In the Self-publishing School, [share], don't just [ask].*

> *In the 90-day Year Group, share your struggles as well as your successes.*

> *Within the Flickr community share YOUR photos.*

> *In the Canon 5D Mark II (DSLR camera) Group: take and share 2 pictures per day.*

I have joined a few Facebook groups related to some online training I have taken. These groups have common expectations of their members. Engage and add value. Sure you can ask questions, but don't just take advice, get ideas, receive input. Give thoughts, share ideas, link to resources, answer questions. Add value to the community.

Here's the challenge for me. It takes all of my attention and then some just to keep up with the groups and with ALL the information that gets thrown around on these sites. They are helpful, but you could lose an entire day filtering through all of the comments.

These mastermind groups have helped me execute. And in the process of engaging in these communities, I have learned a valuable lesson. As I realize my dream, it can monopolize my attention. At times I focus so much on it that I miss the God-given opportunities on the journey to engage with community and add value to the lives of those around me.

The true purpose of our God-infused dreams is to bless people, right? Then, let's make sure to engage along the journey. Let's add value even as we are executing. Let's not isolate ourselves from the very people we hope to influence.

The mastermind groups have actually given me some opportunities to practice what I preach. Here's what I would recommend.

Schedule a Block of Time to Check-In and Then Close It Out

As you realize your dream there is a need to designate time and space for focused work. But remember to set aside time to check in and engage with the community that is helping you on the journey. Share insights you gain through the process. Respond to questions others have about their process. Offer something that might encourage another. Schedule this time. When the time is up, move on. Close the browser. Turn off the notifications and go back to executing your plan.

Online communities are real communities. They connect people with one another around the world. They are actually friendly, helpful, and empowering. They are a valuable resource, based on give and take, receiving and contributing. Everyone has something to offer. Perhaps the church could learn a thing or two from these online communities.

Contribute, Don't Just Take

When you are hyper-focused on realizing your dream, it is tempting to draw as much inspiration and information as possible from these communities. That is our natural MO. I think that's why these groups are so clear at the outset about you engaging in return. You must also consider what the community means to others. You must add value for their sake.

You have much to offer others as they pursue their dreams. Get in there and offer what you have. Share lessons, struggles, insights, resources. Give, don't just take. Inspire others to be courageous, resilient, determined. Share, don't withhold. Tell your story.

When you are finished realizing your dream, it will be a blessing to many people. God intends to multiply your offering. But don't wait that long. Don't put it off until the dream is finally accomplished. There are opportunities to add value right now in the middle of the journey.

TRY THIS

What is one thing you have learned so far in the pursuit of your dream that you could share? Put it out there.

What is a question that you are currently struggling to find an answer to? Ask it in a way that lets others tag along and learn as you find your answer.

What is a process or resource you have discovered or developed in pursuit of your dream that you could share with the people who are following you?

What questions could you answer for someone else?

For the Sake of Your Dream, Exercise Caution in Your Use of Social Media

Social media can be a helpful resource for gaining understanding and support for your dream. Yet, without some helpful boundaries, Facebook, Instagram, Twitter, Snapchat, LinkedIn, YouTube can be the biggest obstacle to the effective execution of your dream. Do yourself a huge favor and establish a consistent plan in managing the electronic pull before you get sucked into its dream-killing vortex.

One dangerous aspect of relying on social media is that it gives us only a snapshot of reality. I acknowledge the virtue of social media. It does allow people to stay in touch with others in a incredibly convenient way. Kind of like a postcard compared to a letter. It may be shallow compared to face-to-face interaction, but that's only if it's used as a substitute. Utilizing these channels as our primary place to get information about people, to stay in touch with family and friends can actually harm, or at the very least, stunt those relationships. To assume you know all about your friend's trip to the Netherlands because you read a couple of posts, is not a safe assumption. These modern-day inventions cannot replace good ol' unhurried conversation.

Assuming we know everything we need to know or can know about any given situation based solely on a social media post has been described as "the paradox effect": "The paradox effect in dating is creating the illusion of having more social engagement, social capital, and popularity, but masking one's true persona. Since some are interfacing digitally more than physically it is much easier to emotionally manipulate others because they are reliant on what I call 'Vanity Validation.' The one you portray on your networks and the true you, for some, creates a double consciousness. Your lauded self on social media is constantly seeking more validation through electronic likes, not life."[59]

Have you noticed how quick you are to judge yourself by how quickly or how frequently people respond to or share your posts? It's a wicked addiction. Think for a moment how this will impact the pursuit of your dream. "Man, I posted a couple of videos on Facebook sharing some thoughts I had been thinking about and I only got a couple of comments, and no shares. They must not be ideas worth pursuing." Suddenly the execution of your dream has inherited another barrier.

"In the latest Match Singles in America study's findings on how social media has impacted people's dating lives, they found that 57% of singles say social media has generated a Fear Of Missing Out (FOMO). Dr. Suzana Flores, author of Facehooked: How Facebook Affects our Emotions, Relationships and Lives explains 'when someone interacts over social media for prolonged periods of time, inevitably they feel compelled to continue to check for updates.

---

59 Clarissa Silva, Social Media's Impact On Self-Esteem, (Huffington Post, Feb. 22, 2017), http://www.huffingtonpost.com/entry/social-medias-impact-on-self-esteem_us_58ade038e4b0d818c4f0a4e4.

I call this the 'Slot Machine Effect' in that when we receive a like or a comment to a post, or when we come across an interesting new post from someone else, we experience what psychologists refer to as intermittent reinforcement—sometimes we get 'rewarded' with an interesting post, and sometimes we are not, but the rewards through external validation of our posts, cause us to remain digitally connected."[60]

If your engagement with social media is interfering with your pursuit of your dream, here's a quick list of remedies:

- Establish Social Media Free zones in your house. *Like, your bedroom, living room, kitchen. The flip side of this idea is to declare ONE area in your house, a place where you can engage.*
- Establish Media Free Times in your day. *Like absolutely no Social Media before 8 am or after 8 pm*
- Schedule time for Social Media on your calendar.
- Turn off your notifications on your phone.
- Bury your apps on page two or following on your phone/tablet.
- Trim your list down to friends you know well and trust.

Here's another truth that will set you free. It's a simple one.

Don't seek out your news on Social Media.

Social media (perhaps ALL news sources) is driven by agendas. It is subjective. Relative. The news it delivers to you is based on your interests and likes and therefore, it is rarely objective. It often filters out facts, which would make it the very opposite of informative. In short, the information in your news feed should not be trusted without verification.

I shared a dramatic news post on Facebook. It touched my heart, and I shared it. It then was reposted by a number of my Facebook friends. It didn't go viral, but it did spread. The next day someone posted an article in response that the same post I sent out had been shared a couple of years ago and was proven to be false. I felt like a schmuck. I had been duped. I am smarter than that!

TRY THIS

How is social media affecting you as you pursue your dream? Is it positive, negative, or neutral?

Can you add your own ideas to the list?

- Establish Social Media Free zones in your house.
- Establish Media Free Times in your day.
- Schedule time for Social Media on your calendar.
- Turn off your notifications on your phone.
- Bury your apps on page two or following on your phone/tablet.
- Trim your list down to friends you know well and trust

Which item(s) on the above list are you willing to try?

Two Social Media Channels Are Enough

Facebook, Snapchat, Instagram, Twitter, LinkedIn, Pinterest, YouTube, Vimeo, Quora... Hey, I'm just getting started! For more on what's out there, check this out.[61]

Who could possibly keep up with all of the social media channels these days and accomplish anything else? Crazy thing is, I have used most of these channels at some point. Here's the point I want to make. Even though I have an account in almost all of these channels, I have not been able to stay up-to-date in all of them. I thought it would be the best idea to build my brand on every social media channel I could. But the results ran counter to my intentions. My attention became scattered and my voice diluted. I've learned that it is better to engage here, there, but definitely not everywhere.

To truly benefit from social media you need to be engaged with others in the channel where you are posting. Too many conversations on too many channels can hurt your productivity and thus diminish the value you offer on those channels. Two seems like a good number to me. Choose two.

61 Curtis Foreman, *10 Types of Social Media and How Each Can Benefit Your Business*, (Hootsuite, June 20, 2017), https://blog.hootsuite.com/types-of-social-media/.

I'm thinking about this on two levels: personal and professional. Think about it. Let's say you have a Twitter account that is used mostly for personal interaction, and a personal Facebook account. You match that with the same channels for professional engagement. How many more do you think you can truly master without losing your mind?

May I suggest investing a little time to consider your options and to determine what will most benefit your dream? Here are some questions to consider:

- What's your purpose for engaging in social media?
- On which sites can you find the people you want to engage?
- Which channels best fit your personality and mode of communication?
- Which age groups should you be targeting with your message?
- Is there someone on your team to whom you could delegate to make this decision and carry out its ongoing execution? In other words, is your time better spent somewhere else? A little caveat here. If you do delegate make sure it is someone you really trust who will represent you well and echo your voice!

If you are going to cast aside what I am saying here, at the very least, invest in some time, and perhaps money to use a service that allows you to see, track, and respond to all your channels from a custom-created dashboard. I would recommend a service like Hootsuite.[62]

62 *Hootsuite,* https://hootsuite.com/.

Evaluate which channels are getting the most engagement. Do some testing. Pay attention to what kinds of posts are creating the most interaction. Recently, I noticed a much higher click-through rate with posts that were personal in nature.

Another area of struggle for me has been whether or not I should allow the social channels that I primarily use to send me notifications. Push notifications may seem to be beneficial in allowing us to stay connected with those who will help our dreams become a reality, but I think that the costs they exact outweigh the benefits. The overwhelming stats tell a story. Consider this. "A Deloitte study in 2016 found that people look at their phones 47 times a day on average; for young people, more like 82. Apple proudly announced in 2013 that 7.4 trillion push notifications had been pushed through its servers. The intervening four years have not reversed the trend."[63]

I concur with David Pierce in his post on *Wired* and would recommend disabling your push notifications. You can always schedule check-in times. This way of getting updates is healthier and more empowering. You should be in control of checking messages, not controlled by them, salivating with every ping.

Consider this: all those notifications were never designed for YOUR benefit. Pierce asserts:

"You'll discover that you don't miss the stream of cards filling your lockscreen, because they never existed for your benefit. They're for brands and developers, methods by which thirsty growth hackers can grab

63 David Pierce, *Turn Off Your Push Notifications. All Of Them.*, (Wired, July 23, 2017), https://www.wired.com/story/turn-off-your-push-notifications/

your attention anytime they want. Allowing an app to send you push
notifications is like allowing a store clerk to grab you by the ear and drag
you into their store. You're letting someone insert a commercial into your
life anytime they want. Time to turn it off."[64]

Take control of your time, your thoughts, your day.

To get a glimpse of how this is currently impacting you, set aside
one week and keep a running list of how many times each day
notifications are taking you off course.

64 *ibid.*

TRY THIS

Here are some questions to consider:

- What's your purpose for engaging in social media?
- On which sites can you find the people you want to engage?
- Which channels best fit your personality and mode of communication?
- Which age groups should you be targeting with your message?
- Is there someone on your team to whom you could delegate to make this decision and carry out its ongoing execution? In other words, is your time better spent somewhere else? A little caveat here. If you do delegate make sure it is someone you really trust who will represent you well and echo your voice!

Write Now. Edit Later

If realizing your dream involves writing, then write now and edit later. Don't do both at the same time.

I am guilty of editing copy and formatting while I write. Not good! Finding the perfect word or phrase or making sure the layout looks presentable has interrupted the flow of my thoughts too many times to count.

If these examples of my writing challenges are not enough to convince you that writing and editing at the same time is a bad idea, then consider these reasons.

Editing while you write can lead to editing BEFORE you write.

I have become so accustomed to writing AND editing simultaneously that there are times I never actually get started with the writing because I am already editing in my head, second-guessing before taking the first step, scolding before allowing myself to get outta line.

Writing and Editing are distinct disciplines using different sides of the brain.

Creative and Analytical. Left and Right. Content and Design. Tug-o-war. Have you ever noticed that there is usually little progress in a tug-o-war? This start-and-stop-back-and-forth dance will only keep you stuck.

Editing while you write is classic multi-tasking.

Most of us don't understand that multitasking is a myth. Studies have proven time and again that we cannot multitask. If we're performing multiple tasks together, we're not doing them at the exact same time. Rather, we are quickly switching back and forth between them. Every time you stop one activity in the middle of it to do a different one you lose time. It takes you longer to get started again. Precious time is lost. I have heard people brag about their ability to multitask. This is not a badge of honor. It is cause for concern. Besides the ineffective use of time, it is proven to be damaging for our brains and our ongoing ability to focus. Just think for a moment what cell phones, email and text notifications, Facebook and Twitter, and stopping to check and respond to every incoming thought or conversation are doing to your productivity, to your quality and depth of thought, to your attitude and mindset. Squirrel! All day long. Squirrel! Editing while you write is like the push notifications we dealt with in Lesson 14 and 26. Turn them off!

Editing while you write impedes progress and creates frustration, which kills the urge to write.

The process of writing can be a difficult challenge in and of itself. Don't compound the difficulty by stopping all the time to self-correct. When I learned to drive, my dad taught me on a stick shift. Honda Accord LX. Loved that car. The first attempts to drive it? Well, let's just say were not smooth. It was painful, learning the rhythm of engaging the gas as I was letting my foot off the clutch. Not just painful for me, either. Sometimes I killed the engine. Editing and writing at the same time is similar. You can kill the engine.

In her post , *7 Ways To Stop Editing While You Work*, Daphne Gray-Grant shares some effective and very practical techniques on how to train your brain to write and not edit at the same time. I love this one.

"Turn off your monitor (or, at least, turn off the screen brightness). Some of my clients gasp when I make this suggestion at workshops, but try it. It works. If your screen is blank then your critical brain will have nothing to do. Note that you must be a touch typist for this to work — otherwise you might get a sentence like: mpr r% jyur yo,r gpt s;; hppf ,rny yp vp,r yp yjr sof pg! Alternatively, you can simply hang a dish towel over your screen."[65]

Do whatever it takes to convince yourself that more careful writing WILL NOT result in a better product. Be relentless in your self-talk when you are writing. Every time you are tempted to stop and

---

65 Daphne Gray-Grant, *7 ways to stop editing while you write,* (Publication Coach), http://www.publicationcoach.com/7-ways-to-stop-editing-while-you-write/.

correct grammar or look for a better word or indent and bold text so that it lays out nicer, STOP! Remind yourself that you writing now and that you will edit later.

TRY THIS

Challenge yourself to write without editing. Write for 5 minutes without worrying about font, spelling, grammar etc.

Notice how this helps you write more, or be more creative. Keep writing.

Try Gray-Grant's blank-screen touch-typing method and see if it eases your self-critiquing impulse.

Hammer Home Your Message

Dreams are never a solo act. They are realized with others, who, if they are going to help you pursue it, will need to catch the excitement of it. And in order for them to catch your vision, you will need to communicate with them effectively.

Drip. Drip. Drip.

Steady. Relentless. Determined. (Repeat).

This approach was good enough for God to deliver the Good News to mankind over centuries. It's good enough for me.

"At many times and in various ways God spoke through the prophets... but in these last days He has spoken to us through His Son" (Hebrews 1:1).

There is no IF you need to be heard. What you have to say DOES NEED to be heard, full stop. The world is blessed with your message.

So, SINCE YOU WANT TO BE HEARD, use Hebrews 1:1 as a template for communicating your message:

Many times... Timing and Repetition

Be willing to repeat. So many times we communicators stop when we think, "they've already heard this." Hearing does not equal understanding, grasping or owning. Hearing can mean in one ear and out the other. Only that which gets repeated will have a chance to stick.

Various ways… Methodology and Tools

Think of communicating as a toolbox of mediums. Written word, spoken word, stories, perspectives, images, video, posts, blogs, letters, notes, conversations, formal presentations, sermons, speeches, clips from movies, GIFs, music, lyrics, poetry….use them all. Rummage through your tool box and pick one out. Don't expect to get it right the first time. Experiment and tinker.

And, right now (these last days)…embody it, live it Be willing to share HOW you are living out what you are sharing. Share the positive results AND the struggles. Show people HOW you apply your message in your own life. Remember, Vulnerability =Validity

Think this way in your delivery: Omnipresent AND Omnipotent Volume AND Value. Not just a lot of stuff, but your **best** stuff. Not simply quantity, but quality. Don't barrage people with noise; inspire them with noteworthy And here is a key thing to remember: if you want to be heard you must be willing to be disregarded. *"….how many times I would have gathered you to myself, but you would not." –* Jesus (Matthew 23:37) *"The city who kills the prophets and stones God's messengers…" Luke 13:34* Yet, Jesus rode on. If you want to be heard, you cannot linger. You cannot hold back your insight until you are assured of acceptance. You must be willing to face rejection.

Think of all the great ideas that were originally rejected.

The telephone, the computer, the automobile, the airplane...

The Gospel. Where would we be without these gifts?

Frequently, those who need to hear the message many times and in various ways are themselves DREAMERS. As I sit here typing this lesson in my home office, I notice across the room that my light-up message board says, "I believe you can do this!" A message from my great encourager, Amy. Another word again from another medium, another vantage point, a message that keeps me going.

Immediately to the right of that sign are a collection of 40 post-it-notes I placed on the closet door reminding me of what's most important. I glance at them occasionally. Pull one off and really soak it in sometimes. Early in the morning. Affirming who I am apart from my dream. These are messages I need to hear again and again.

Drip. Drip. Drip.

TRY THIS

What message do you have that you want to be heard? Who have you told? Who else can you tell?

How are you living out the message? What story from your own life do you have to share? If you are struggling, who can you share your struggle with?

How can you drip your message this week? Make a list of opportunities. Conversations, social media, video snippets, stories, notes, speeches, etc.

Turn the Intuitive into the Intentional

People will not be able to do what you do if you don't show them *how* to do what you do. And you will not be able to show them *how* if you haven't thought through each step in your process. Replication begins with clear, methodical articulation.

Caveat: If you want to keep what you do a secret, stored away high on a shelf so that only you can do it, then by all means, skip this chapter. But if the idea of sharing what you do for the benefit of others or even for the sake of your own legacy appeals to you, then please pay heed.

It is almost a certainty that if your dream has been given to you by God, it will grow. At some level your dream will demand that others participate. That's the way the Kingdom of God works.

Pause for a moment. Think about something that you do that you think would be valuable to pass on. Pick something. Pay particular attention to the things you do quite naturally. The things you do intuitively may not come as easily for others. Be comprehensive in your articulation. What you do is your gift to the world. It doesn't take much effort for you because you are naturally good at it.

For example, over the years writing my sermon series became intuitive. One day I fielded the question, "How do you write a sermon series?" And all I could offer was an ineffectual "I don't know, I just write them, I guess."

A few years ago I decided to let others in on the preaching fun. I was preparing to train our Preacher's Learning Community to write a sermon series when I discovered that what I had been doing instinctively all these years was very difficult to explain to my guys. I had never considered how I write a sermon series. It was ironic: I had never put into words how I put my thoughts into words. I realized that I had work to do. What followed was an afternoon of me sitting down and committing to paper a careful, thoughtful, step-by-step sequencing of the steps involved in my writing process.

It took a conscious decision to describe something I did intuitively so that someone else could do it deliberately.

I'm glad to report that my labor bore fruit. I now share the sermon series writing privilege with others.

You can do this too!

Move from
[intuitive…instinctive…automatic]

to
[conscious, deliberate, thought out].

Take something that has become intuitive and break it down. Step by step, habit-by-habit, ingredient-by-ingredient. Have fun watching others do what you do.

One of the major reasons we are not seeing growth in our churches is because we are not teaching people to do what we do.

Use this simple, three-step formula to move from intuitive to intentional.

Figure Out What You Are Doing

Identify something you have been doing for so long that it has become natural and almost effortless. Could this benefit others if you shared it?

Name It

In simple, concrete terms, write down each step in the process you want to share. The more intuitive the activity is for you, the more difficult it may be to describe the process. Don't be put off by that. Stay with it. Think it through. What are the steps? 1-2-3

Share It

Give others the privilege of doing what you are doing. Share the opportunity with them. Paul tells young Timothy to "entrust" his message to reliable people (2 Timothy 2:2). Let others try. Show them what you wrote down. Better yet, *show* them how to do it. Let them watch you. Then let them try while you watch and offer guidance.

Anything can be taught using this three-step formula.

Here's a rapid-fire off-the-top-of-my-head list: Managing finances, praying out loud, having a "quiet time", engaging in conversations with strangers, riding a bike, choosing healthy foods at the grocery store, exercising, setting the table, cleaning up after dinner, reading the Bible, preaching, teaching, running a backyard VBS, video editing, worship leading, being able to recognize how God is working, prayer walking, serving in the community, sales, cooking, creating a website, recording a screencast, writing a story, playing the trumpet, overcoming fear, dreaming a big dream, & executing.

TRY THIS

Name one area in your leadership today that you would like to share with someone else.

Once you've identified it, try out the three-step formula.

1. Figure out what you are doing.
2. Name it.
3. Share it.

Love Reduces Distance and Overcomes Gripping Fear

There is an intimate connection between you and your dream. Your dream is alive. Thus far, you may have discovered that FEAR and APATHY pose the greatest obstacles in the process of realizing your dream.

So, how do we move forward in pursuit of our dream when fear is a reality?

Enact love.

We've all experienced relational conflict. Some of us have suffered deep pain. Some of us have inflicted deep pain. Some of these injuries have been intentional, some unintentional. Doesn't matter. Pain is pain. One of the common responses to this kind of pain is to ignore it, to avoid it. But time does not heal all wounds. Absence does not always make the heart grow fonder. Sometimes it's the very opposite.

I think the following equation is just as true as the platitudes:

Increased distance *from* + Increased time *away* = **Fear**

The sum total is an ugly disposition.

> *I doubt. I am anxious. I worry. I dread. I am*
> *apprehensive. I am uncertain. I hesitate. I exist as a*
> *nervous and skeptical person, both with God and with*
> *those from whom I am distanced.*

When I avoid a person or situation for an extended period, one of two things eventually will increase: fear or apathy. Fear leads to avoidance. Avoidance leads to fear. It's a vicious cycle. We steer clear of interactions in order to escape any conflict. Apathy leads to meanness. We become callous and hard. Crusted over by our judgement, we turn the ones we are distanced from into monsters.

The only thing that will begin to bridge that gap is to enact genuine love. The chasm will never be spanned from a distance. In order to have a chance at closing the wound, someone has to take the first step. Waiting for the other is not productive. And waiting is another instance of judgment. I wait because I know they are wrong. I wait because it is their responsibility to act in love, not mine. And so the wicked cycle continues. Meanwhile, the other party is probably thinking the same thing!

"There is no fear in love. But perfect love drives out fear" (New International Version, 1 John 4:18). And perfect love is not a feeling or sentiment, or vague philosophy. It is an act.

> "For God so loved the world that **He sent** His one
> and only Son.... He did not come to judge the
> world, but to save the world" (John 3:16 & 17).

> "And the Word **became flesh** and **dwelt among us**...full of grace and truth" (English Standard Version, John 1:14).

God's love is the perfect antidote to our fear. While we were far away in our fear and in our judgment, God initiated a perfect act of love. It was, and is, THE perfect act of love. Scripture describes us as enemies of God. While we were still His enemies, He sacrificed His Son. He gave His most generous gift. He took the giant step to bridge the gap. He stepped into our world knowing full well that many would reject His offer. That knowledge did not stop Him. He did it anyway. He took the initiative at great risk that many would misinterpret His move. Didn't matter. He initiated anyway. And with this act of confidence, He forgave me, you, all of us. He took my place and initiated all of the times I have been petrified and unmoved. He is my substitute. And it is this waterfall of grace that enables me to go and do likewise in my broken relationships with others.

God's love, manifested in the perfect gift of Jesus, is the enacted love that moves me. Supernaturally, almost magically, it propels me. And He gets all the praise. It's His. It's always His. Because He has always taken the first step.

And then I can simply repay in kind, moving toward Him. It is not my place to worry about how my move will be interpreted or received. It is my place simply to step. Because He stepped.

Because of God's foundational, initiating love, I have broken the shackles of fear (Romans 8:15). This is a far greater equation than the one that began this lesson.

God's love for me + His initiating move = **Confidence**

The sum total is a pleasing readiness.

> *I depend (on God). I am assured. I trust. I anticipate.*
> *I am bold. I am secure. I seek. I live as a composed and*
> *believing person, with God and with those from whom*
> *I am distanced.*

Compare the two descriptions. What do you notice?

Here's the most amazing revelation of this lesson. You can look at your dreams as a relationship. Reposition you dream from an inanimate thing to a person with whom you relate. Think of it as having flesh and blood. Think a moment about how fear has solidified as it pertains to your dream. Increased distance from + Increased time away has made that fear like concrete!

So, as you carry on with your dream realization, don't forget to get back to the basics, which are never out of style or too elementary to revisit. God's love for you + His initiating move is the formula to sustain the process. Because it will take **confidence** to realize your dream.

TRY THIS

As you reflect on today's lesson, take some time in your journal, and let God write in it.

What words or descriptions would you like Him to write to depict your ability to realize your dream?

As you think about a relational conflict that you are experiencing, which of the words that God has written in your journal seems to be the most relevant today?

As you think about any relational conflict that you may be experiencing with your dream, which of God's descriptions of you do you want to hold on to?

Talk to God about these things.

Concluding Thoughts

I'm a *14er*. The title is a badge of honor given to anyone who climbs a 14,000 ft. mountain peak. There are 58 14,000 ft. + mountain peaks in the great state of Colorado. More than any other state.

On a family vacation to Breckenridge, CO, my daughter Abbey and I did some research and discovered Quandary Peak. Eight miles south of Breckenridge, Quandary is one of the 14,ooo ft. peaks. 14,265 feet, to be exact. We first heard of Quandary in a discussion with a local. "It's a great climb for first-timers." Jumping online and reading about the trailhead, we determined to give it a try.

Being in Colorado you get the bug to hike. I'm not a hiker. Abbey, on the other hand, loves it. But at this point in her young life she had not had many opportunities to indulge the passion.

We would take the journey together on a Friday. We had a couple of days to get ready. Packing snacks, getting the appropriate shoes, clothes, backpacks with hydration bladders, even taking a few smaller hikes to get our bodies ready were among the items on our checklist.

The excitement built as we got closer to Friday. It was increasingly difficult to sleep as we approached the day. We were both doing something we had never done before. Abbey had dreamt of this for awhile. The thought was new to me. We wondered, would we see mountain goats? Would it be cold at the peak? Did we have the right kind of clothes? Would we have enough time to get up and down before sunset? Were we in good enough shape? Would my knees handle the relentless pressure? What would we see? Would the weather be nice? Tossing and turning Thursday night, the pressure to try and get some sleep had the opposite effect.

In spite of nervousness and doubt, we got up early on Friday morning. Pulling our gear together and looking at each other pensively, we silently kept moving forward. We were going to do this thing! It would be an adventure.

We made it to the trailhead, got our stuff together, took deep breaths, and began our ascent.

Ten minutes into the hike, we had to stop to catch our breath! The combination of excitement and a rapid incline had already caught up with us. We looked at each other and wondered if we were nuts. *10 minutes in and we're stopping?* Our research had told us that with a steady pace it would take us four hours. *What were we thinking? Should we keep going?*

We had some trail mix, drank some water, and carried on. On the way we saw the tree line disappear. We saw and interacted with some awesome mountain goats, met people from Wisconsin, passed some who were slower than us, had others pass us. As we got closer, others were coming down the mountain. Everyone would say, "Keep going. You're almost there. It's worth it." Occasionally we would stop to just take in the beauty, snap a few pictures, have another snack. Then we would start climbing again.

Quandary provides an interesting challenge. When you are nearing the final third of the climb you can see the peak. This is a good thing. Except that it appears to be closer than it really is. The climb should come with a warning label, the opposite of the one on side mirrors: "Peak appears closer than it is." *We should be there by now. Why is this taking so long? Will we ever get there? Do we have enough time? This is killing me!* Abbey finally said something about all my sighing, eye-rolling, and moaning and groaning. (She's so impatient sometimes; I don't know where she gets it...)

Climbing one boulder after another, quads burning, lungs straining, the encouragement from those descending swelled in our ears above the throbbing of our heartbeats. *We were almost there! Keep going. We're going to make it!*

And then, there it was. The peak. We had climbed our way to the top. We had reached the pinnacle. Breathtaking. We stood in complete awe. Snapped selfies, posing with our arms extended to the heavens. The moment made me feel small... yet valuable. I looked down at my cell phone and realized that I had coverage! So...(vulnerability alert) I called my mother. And we shared the moment. It was an emotional experience. Abbey and I enjoyed lunch together at 14,265 feet. Just my sweet Abbey and me. Oh, and the other 20 or so people who made up our new Quandary Peak Community. Then, after about an hour of taking it all in, we began our descent. What a day! I won't soon forget it.

This is what it looks like to *Listen*, *Trust*, and *Envision*.

This is what it looks like to *Obey, Persevere, Share*.

Lesson Checklist

Part 1: Dream Sparks

Part 2: Realization Strategies

☐ Lesson 10   Busyness as an Indicator of Productivity Is a Myth

☐ Lesson 11   Leadership Is Lonely, yet I Am Never Alone

☐ Lesson 12   Unsettled Leaders Are Unsettled for Many Reasons

☐ Lesson 13   Stop Worrying About Outcomes

☐ Lesson 14   There Will Always Be Distractions

☐ Lesson 15   Stuck? Change It Up

☐ Lesson 16   When You Want to Change, Strategies Are More Helpful Than Willpower

☐ Lesson 17   In Addressing Bad Habits, Think "Replace," Not "Remove"

☐ Lesson 18   Behavioral Change Requires PRACTICE (Repetition over Time)

☐ Lesson 19   I Don't Need a New Assignment

☐ Lesson 20   When You Read, 'Fear Not,' Know That God Is with You

☐ Lesson 21   The Plan Forward Begins with One Step, the NEXT One

☐ Lesson 22   Embrace the Paradox: Everything Is Not on My Shoulders, and, Everything Changes When I Do

☐ Lesson 23   My Broken Spaces Are Not to Be Covered Up or Compensated For

☐ Lesson 24   Add Value

☐ Lesson 25   For the Sake of Your Dream, Exercise Caution in Your Use of Social Media

☐ Lesson 26   Two Social Media Channels Are Enough

☐ Lesson 27   Write Now. Edit Later

☐ Lesson 28   Hammer Home Your Message

☐ Lesson 29   Turn the Intuitive into the Intentional

☐ Lesson 30   Love Reduces Distance and Overcomes Gripping Fear

Appendix

The Enneagram is a tool to help individuals understand their unique personality. It is an eerily accurate personality typing system that classifies nine different personality types. While no personality test or system can tell us all we need to know about a human being, the Enneagram is a powerful tool in one's work toward greater self-understanding.

I'm an Enneagram Type Four. Read more about the nine Enneagram types here:

https://www.enneagraminstitute.com/type-descriptions/

History

https://www.enneagraminstitute.com/the-traditional-enneagram/

https://www.enneagramspectrum.com/173/history-of-the-enneagram/

How the Enneagram Works

https://www.enneagraminstitute.com/how-the-enneagram-system-works

App

Enneapp, https://www.enneaapp.com/

Books

The Road Back To You: An Enneagram Journey to Self-Discovery by Ian Morgan Cron and Suzanne Stabile, IVP Books (October 4, 2016)

The Enneagram: A Christian Perspective by Richard Rohr & Andreas Ebert, The Crossroad Publishing Company; 1st US Edition 1st Printing edition (September 1, 2001)

Personality Types: Using The Enneagram for Self-Discovery by Don Richard Riso, Russ Hudson, Mariner Books; Revised, Subsequent edition (October 29, 1996)

Testimonials

"Jeff's work is not just a great book, it is a great work of facilitation. Whether you need a spark to discover your dream or better strategies for executing the dream you already have, this book is the help you are seeking. Consider Jeff's book your toolbox for getting better as a leader. And consider each of the lessons he provides to be the tools you need for unleashing a whole new era of clarity and effectiveness for you and your people."

—Greg Finke, executive director of Dwelling 1:14
and author of the "Joining Jesus" series

"For every book I have read that inspired... yet left me motionless, I have read another that directed... yet found me emotionless. In Fear Not Dream Big & Execute, Jeff Meyer successfully stokes a raging God-fire of mission from the cooling embers of calling, especially for those suffering the winds of Sunday-to-Sunday survival. Street-level practicality walks hand in hand with rare-air creativity in every lesson, challenging the reader to be more, not just do more. I can easily see this book being a go-to leadership resource on my bedside table for years of ministry to come."

—Bryan Rose, Auxano Lead Navigator, co-founder of Family Younique

"A gifted thought partner and creative catalyst, Jeff Meyer invites us to explore the many ways in which we blur our vision and cripple our momentum. Equipped with this generous offering of insights and exercises, you'll learn to discern your dream, and protect it from your own ego's insistence to stay safe and play small. As for the well-meaning yet disrupting, even discouraging agendas that others hold for you and your vision, Part 1: Lesson 13 gives wise guidance on how to release your expectations of support and approval from them, with love. If your habit is to downsize your dreams to fit your perception of what's possible, Fear Not Dream Big & Execute will empower both the dreaming and doing in your life, linking you to God's immeasurably grand plan."

—Lynn Schoener, Owner, Executive & Team Coach
Coaching Creative Change

"Some books are written to be read, others to be experienced. This book is like sitting with a sage advisor bringing clarity and challenge for the path forward. If you want loving encouragement backed by practical tools then this experience is for you."

—Ben and Kate Griffin, Directors of LINC Minneapolis

"Pursuing a dream can feel either too abstract or like one more obligation for an already busier-than-I-should-be working mom with an ever-growing to-do list. This book shows us how having dreams and pursuing them can and should inspire, taking us from a mindset of "ought to" to "get to," launching us from a world of obligation to a world of passion, opportunity, and adventure. This book sparked a dream in me, and I can't wait to see what God does with it."

—Katie Ignatowski, wife, mother, and executive legal counsel

"I was hooked early and hard. In reading 'Part 1: Lesson 18: I Will Not Overcome First World Consumeristic Christianity,' I realized (for the first time) the struggles and fatigue in which I was navigating life were completely in my control. I have chased the American Dream hard for many years. Yet, I had never felt farther away from it. The emptiness has been eating at me. Today I realize I am pursuing the wrong dream. I will always feel empty chasing the American Dream regardless of what it produces. My thirst will only be quenched through Jesus Christ."

—Loren Brockhouse, SVP Strategy at Businessolver

"God has given us so much creativity and so much permission. A gifted leader and thinker like Jeff is the perfect guide to help us pursue our biggest dreams by giving us practical questions, tools, and steps to follow. If you are hoping to make a big impact in the world for the kingdom of God, this book is perfect for you."

—Adam Griffin Lead Pastor of Eastside Community Church, a church plant of The Village Church in Dallas Texas

"Perhaps you feel you are merely surviving, perpetually dreaming that there must be something more. Perhaps you are thriving, having discovered and living your vision. Or perhaps you are somewhere in between; you have a dream but feel stuck, unable to make it happen. No matter where you are in this spectrum, you will find inspiration and insight in this thoughtful Biblically-grounded book that will help you discover, execute, and really live your God-given vision. Along with inspiration, this book is replete with practical tools to help you make your dream your reality ... and stay focused. Dive into this accessible tool and you will be inspired to dream BIG, be bold, discover, and fulfill your vision by living out your unique gifts and passions."

—Cheryl Marting, Communication and Team Building Specialist

"As a mom and entrepreneur, I find the style of this book to be ideal: Succinct, focused lessons that can be read quickly but encourage further reflection. 'Lesson 25: Without Relentless Singularity Mission Creep Is Inevitable' identifies a crucial challenge in executing a big dream -- losing sight of our mission. We must be intentional in relying on Scripture and prayer to ensure that the mission we are following is the one God has set before us. 'The enemy of your soul is the master of mission creep.' Thanks for the insight, Jeff!"

—Kirsten Adshead, founder of <u>motherbility.com</u>

"Jeff is a skillful navigator who takes us on a journey to a more thoughtful and purposeful life not only reminding us that dreams are a reflection of our heart but creating a pathway to follow."

—David Putman, Author and Lead Navigator with Auxano

"Jeff has written a book that will motivate you to get in touch with what you really want to do and go for it. You will find this book challenging and inspiring. He includes reflective questions at the end of each chapter to help you take the ideas presented and apply it to your life. He wants to spark a movement of kingdom dreamers. Would you like to join him?"

—*James C. Galvin, Ed.D., President, Galvin & Associates, Inc.*

"From the outside a walk with the Lord can look like God has us in a grand field where his sheep play and feed in the fresh green grass and drink by cool waters. Reality is, there are some days where that pasture is a wet, soggy, hill side where the shepherd can't help but get his boots so stuck in the slop as he walks, that they literally can get pulled right off of his feet. I love that this book is meant to help shepherds/pastors/lay people see our walk with God for what it is. Ministry is not clean, a walk on God's path is not easy and there are days when it feels like you're stuck in the mud.

I read this book and looked at it as a little help for me on those days when I am stuck. The lessons, images, and exercises are meant to take hold of individually on the days when you need to be picked up and moved to dry ground. That is what I found in this book. It is a book of hope and inspiration to give me a push, or a nudge to get going again as my wheels are spinning in the mud."

—*Pastor Anthony Kobak, The Hanover Lutheran Church*

"I am thrilled to have a Christian resource that challenges believers to throw off fear and to courageously dream and live as our Creator intended. It is both inspiring and practical. It is a tool I intend to use for myself and to share."

—*Anneke Hudson, author, Bevilacqua:*
Christian meditations for young women

"We see gifted leaders come to PLI who have settled for too little. For too long. We frequently watch them breakout. And breakthrough. Jeff Meyer extends a hand to you in this book to breakout. To witness breakthrough! We highly recommend this book to you. You'll be encouraged. You'll be challenged. You'll be repeatedly invited to 'try this' and discover the steps to acting on what you've sensed God placed in your heart some time ago."

—Gail and Jock Ficken, PLI Executive Leaders

Thank You Very Much!

I appreciate you reading my book *"Fear Not, Dream Big, & Execute: Tools To Spark Your Dream And Ignite your Follow-Through"*

If you found value in this book, would you please write a helpful review with your favorite book distributor, or on Amazon?

Thanks in advance for all your feedback. I wish you great joy in the pursuit of your dream!

— **Jeff Meyer**

LOVED THE BOOK?
Has a dream been sparked?

We've made the next three steps easy for you to
#moveforwardanyway in the pursuit of your dream.

(1) Turn your fuzzy dream or seemingly disconnected ideas into a High-resolution Dream that inspires you to take action.

▶ **Schedule your FREE 30-minute Discovery Call**

Scan this code to
get on the calendar

(2) Move your High-resolution Dream from your head into an actionable plan. Join the Dream Accelerator community.

▶ **Go to *info.jeffmeyer.org/dream-accelerator* for more information.**

(3) Help others spark and realize their dreams. Gift the book to a friend through Amazon (and be sure to leave a review)!

JEFF MEYER
Founder of the *Dream Accelerator*
jeff@jeffmeyer.org
www.fearnotdreambig.com

#fearnotdreambig | Find me on Social media **@jeffmeyer22**

10688599R00199

Made in the USA
Monee, IL
01 September 2019